THE ENCOUNTER SERIES

1. *Virtue—Public and Private*
2. *Unsecular America*
3. *Confession, Conflict, and Community*
4. *Democracy and the Renewal of Public Education*

Democracy and the Renewal of Public Education

Essays by

Richard A. Baer, Jr.
Charles L. Glenn
Rockne M. McCarthy
James W. Skillen
Paul C. Vitz

Edited and with a foreword by
Richard John Neuhaus

WILLIAM B. EERDMANS PUBLISHING COMPANY
GRAND RAPIDS, MICHIGAN

Published by Wm. B. Eerdmans Publishing Co.
in cooperation with
The Rockford Institute Center on Religion & Society

Copyright © 1987 by Wm. B. Eerdmans Publishing Co.
255 Jefferson Ave. S.E., Grand Rapids, Mich. 49503

All rights reserved
Printed in the United States of America

Library of Congress Cataloging-in-Publication Data:

Democracy and the renewal of public education.

(The Encounter series ; 4)
1. Education—United States—Aims and objectives—
Congresses. 2. Public schools—United States—Congresses.
3. Democracy—Congresses. I. Baer, Richard A.
II. Neuhaus, Richard John. III. Series.
LA217.D45   1987   371'.01'0973   86-32808

ISBN 0-8028-0204-4

Contents

Foreword   vii

Richard A. Baer, Jr.
   American Public Education
   and the Myth of Value Neutrality   1

Charles L. Glenn
   "Molding" Citizens   25

Rockne M. McCarthy
   Public Schools and Public Justice:
   The Past, the Present, and the Future   57

James W. Skillen
   Changing Assumptions in the Public Governance of Education:
   What Has Changed and What Ought to Change   86

Paul C. Vitz
   A Study of Religion and Traditional Values
   in Public School Textbooks   116

Tracy Early
   The Story of an Encounter   141

Participants   169

Foreword

If you're starting out to renew something, you should know what it is that you want to renew. That seems a sound principle. There is another maxim that has gained currency in recent years: "If it ain't broke, don't fix it." One is not likely to get much of an argument today by claiming that education—or at least a large part of what we call education—is broken. A considerable number of people, not least professional educators, think education is not doing what it's supposed to do, although the same people are not at all agreed on just what it is that education is supposed to do.

The people you will meet in this book are leading educators and analysts of education. They share a keen awareness that something has gone terribly wrong with education in America, and they share a history of advocating some proposals for what might be done. In one way or another, the proposals meet around the idea of "democratizing" education. And, in their understanding of democracy, "choice" has a central role. Especially with respect to values and beliefs, these people say, the part that parents and families play in education must be strengthened. In that process, they believe, teachers too would be empowered to do what really good teachers most want to do—namely, to communicate to children the excitement of the ideas and virtues by which we aspire to live together.

As the title says, the thing that needs renewing is *public* education. But to undertand what this means, we have to examine again what we mean by "public." Some readers may think this book very radical, but the examination it undertakes has occupied the attention of Americans for well over a hundred years. The questions involved were joined most intensively in the middle of the nineteenth century when the "common school movement" succeeded in "establishing" government control over "public" education. The conclusions reached at that time, this book suggests, are no longer appropriate a century later. The chapters by Charles Glenn and Rockne McCarthy, in particular, tell the story of how the debate was joined in the nineteenth century. Now a new national debate is underway, and I expect the reader will be surprised at how the arguments that were advanced then are, in substance and tone, strikingly similar to the arguments being made now.

"New occasions teach new duties," as the hymn says, and that is undoubtedly right. But to understand both the occasion and the duty, we need to be instructed by how other people have perceived their occasions and duties. The previous century's perceptions led to our present situation, in which "public" schools are sharply distinguished from "private" schools, especially from "religious" (read "sectarian") schools. In fact, those who today talk about empowering parents and teachers for real educational choice are sometimes seen as enemies of "public education." That is a grievous misperception which can be sustained only by a narrow and distorted definition of what "public" means with respect to education.

The conference that produced this book was held at the Princeton Club in New York City, a place redolent with the early history of the American republic. It is a good place to ask the kinds of questions the founders asked about the meaning of freedom and democratic governance. It is a good place to ask, as the distinguished legal scholar Stephen Arons asked, what would have happened in subsequent First Amendment law if the nineteenth century had viewed education as "communication," which is therefore constitutionally protected from government control and censorship. It is a good place to examine the curious, even bizarre, directions that censorship has taken, as illuminated by Dr. Paul Vitz's chapter on textbooks.

Finally, the perspectives and proposals advanced in this book are visionary but not utopian. They recognize that education will always be a problem, especially as it touches upon the values by which we would order our common life. But it will be less of a problem, these experts contend, if we move toward a more expansive definition of "public" and if we sincerely act upon the devotion to democratic pluralism that most Americans profess. The fresh ways of thinking about education represented here will not become public policy tomorrow. This is a book that intends to point out directions, to set forth principles, to propose paradigms, to provoke experiment. It envisions not revolutionary change but incremental, careful, even cautious change. The one thing that is certain is that we cannot rest content with the answers given in the nineteenth century if we wish to bring about a genuine renewal of public education. Those answers have now played themselves out, and artificially sustaining them can only aggravate the crisis of contemporary education. Yet, if we are to arrive at better answers for the twentieth century, we must be as courageous as our nineteenth-century forebears were in asking the hard questions about what education is and what education is for in a democratic society.

The conference was sponsored by the Center on Religion and Society, and we are grateful to the Department of Education and its director of issues analysis, Jack Klenk, and to James Skillen of the Association for Public Justice for making available to us the materials that provided the basis for the conference discussion. I am personally indebted to John Howard and Allan Carlson, my colleagues at the Rockford Institute, and, as always, to Paul Stallsworth, my associate at the Center.

Richard John Neuhaus

THE ROCKFORD INSTITUTE
CENTER ON RELIGION AND SOCIETY,
NEW YORK CITY

American Public Education and the Myth of Value Neutrality

Richard A. Baer, Jr.

Next to raising standards and striving for academic excellence, few topics are currently of greater interest in education than the question of how to deal with values and religion in public schools. The subject is a large one, though, and I have no room here to treat a number of its important aspects. I've chosen not to try to deal with such things as the question of how peer pressure affects value formation in schools, for instance, or what might be gained by less segregation of children according to age, or by more interesting and varied contact between children and adults in the workplace. Nor will I be addressing the critically important subject of how a teacher functions as a role model, or how schools develop a particular ambience or character, or the importance of enlightened and fair discipline in schools. Beyond this, I will note only in passing such things as the introduction of methods such as Values Clarification and Decision Making (which have been heralded as neutral and noncoercive ways to deal with values in public schools) and the sorts of bias found in almost all of the sex education curricula I have seen.

I will be treating these other issues only peripherally because I want to focus on several *structural* characteristics of our public schools and on some basic assumptions widely held by educators that directly affect the place of values and religion in these schools. I want to examine these with a particular concern for justice and fairness in light of the First Amendment and in relation to our historic concern for liberty and freedom of conscience.

The current national debate over education so far has been too limited in scope. By focusing almost entirely on how to rehabilitate our present system of public schools rather than asking fundamental questions about the structure and basic assumptions that make the system what it is, we have cut ourselves off from new possibilities that might vastly increase not only freedom in teaching and learning but also the quality of education. Indeed, it seems more and more obvious to a small minority of educational theorists that problems such as the censorship of school textbooks and the place of religion and values in public schools simply cannot be resolved adequately within present structures and within the framework of assumptions held by a majority of professional educators.

Inasmuch as my remarks will be critical of our current public school system, I should note that I am well aware of the many impressive achievements of our public schools in teaching and learning, in helping us as a nation to move toward racial justice and equality of opportunity. And although our schools sometimes leave much to be desired in the way of educational quality, I shall have little to say about teachers as such. My quarrel is with the structure of the system, not mainly with the people who operate it. Teaching is an honorable, fulfilling, and at times a very tough and unappreciated profession. And in return for the little we are willing to pay many teachers, we more often than not get better than we deserve in the way of hard work, dedication, and good results.

I am myself a product of the public schools, and I teach in a tax-supported college at Cornell University. Thus in a very real sense I speak as one who stands within the system, not as an outsider taking potshots from a position of security and noninvolvement.

CRITICAL STRUCTURAL FEATURES OF AMERICA'S PUBLIC SCHOOLS

Let me begin by pointing to four structural features of our public schools that deeply affect the way we deal with values and religion in public education.

1. *America's public school system is a government monopoly with a captive student audience.* Although in theory people have the right to choose private schools for their children, in actuality, apart from Catholic parochial schools and other privately subsidized systems, only the affluent have the option of choosing for their children alternative private schools with values and practices more closely suited to their own basic beliefs. Most parents are not willing—and many are not able

in any case—to assume the heroic and often crushing expense of private education; they simply *have* to send their children to public schools. The system is monopolistic in that only government schools are eligible to receive tax dollars for general support. We have what Professor Stephen Arons of the University of Massachusetts has described as "a system of school finance that provides free choice for the rich and compulsory socialization for everyone else."[1]

2. *America's public schools are government schools.* In a strict sense, public school teachers, administrators, and other employees are representatives or agents of the government—and hence the public school can appropriately be called a "government school." But the term is also appropriate for another reason. The dichotomy between public and private schools is essentially misleading. After all, taken as a whole, private elementary and secondary schools are in a sense as open to the general public as are public schools. And specifically, they are not as a class significantly less well integrated racially, socially, or economically than are the public schools. Admittedly, this is in large part because of the splendid record of Catholic parochial schools, but the point is nonetheless worth noting. As John E. Coons of the University of California (Berkeley) Law School has recently pointed out, most of our better public schools are "functionally private in the sense that access is closely linked to the family's purchasing power and thus to its ability to exit [neighborhoods with poor schools].... What we call public schools," he continues, "are in fact geographically exclusive schools."[2] It is a serious mistake to equate the word *public* with "government-sponsored" or "government-financed." To be fully accurate, we should describe schools as either "government schools" or "nongovernment schools" rather than as "public" or "private."

3. *It is a myth that America's system of government schools constitutes a network of local schools or that these schools function in loco parentis.* Over the years, America's public schools have increasingly come to be run by state and federal governmental agencies rather than by local school boards. State boards of education have become more and more powerful in determining the curriculum, selecting textbooks, and certifying teachers. And the federal government has increasingly

---

1. Arons, *Compelling Belief: The Culture of American Schooling* (New York: McGraw-Hill, 1983), p. 211.

2. Coons, "A Question of Access," *Independent School*, February 1985, p. 6.

required local schools to follow its mandates in noncurricular matters in order to qualify for much-needed federal aid.

So it is wrong to suppose that local communities or parents control local schools. Twenty-two states choose textbooks on a statewide basis. In New York State, it is basically the State Board of Regents that controls the high school curriculum. Schools of education exercise powerful influence over curricula, and parents have learned to their dismay that it is exceedingly difficult if not impossible to counteract pressure from the state to incorporate courses in sex education and Values Clarification programs into the local school curriculum. The federally funded National Institute of Education exercises substantial power over what kind of research on education will be undertaken, and increasingly state and federal courts determine what schools may and may not do in a broad range of curricular and noncurricular matters.

4. *America's government-monopoly school system cannot rightly be described as a "marketplace of ideas."* When classical libertarian theorists talked and wrote about censorship, they for the most part had in mind a marketplace of ideas analogous to the popular image of the economic market. They maintained that we all ought to be free to pursue our own goals and choose things to read or listen to that reflect our own values or values we want to learn about. All individuals in this market should be free to "sell" ideas by saying or printing what they want, and others should be free to "buy" these ideas or not, just as they choose. In such a context, censorship is a very serious matter, for it disrupts the marketplace. Ideas no longer flow freely, and the system breaks down.

Media critics of Catholic and fundamentalist Christian "censors" have mistakenly assumed that the public schools are also a genuine marketplace of ideas. The actual situation, however, is that all of the textbooks, library books, curricula, and films in these schools are preselected by teachers, state agencies, and other professional educators and bureaucrats. And publishers strongly influence this process as well. Thus in a real sense textbooks and curricula are censored before parents ever get involved in the process. As every man or woman who decides to marry knows (or should know), to say Yes to one person is to say No to all others. And indeed, any act of selection is simultaneously an act of exclusion. But this has a special significance in the context of a government-monopoly school system, with its captive student audience, for it underscores the fact that the school system in its entirety is a kind of closed forum and not a genuine marketplace of ideas at all.

I realize that I have not done any sort of justice to the complexity of the issues of values and censorship in this brief discussion. I simply want to establish what I take to be a basic problem in much of the discussion centering on these issues. And I would add that the real problem with respect to elementary and secondary schools—that is, schools that typically serve minors—is not that such preselection or censorship takes place but rather that it is government rather than the parents that controls the process. The great libertarian thinker John Stuart Mill argued that it is proper for teachers to direct the schooling of minors, since full freedom is appropriate only for people "in the maturity of their faculties." Freedom for minors has to be limited for their own good—to prevent them from harming themselves. Nevertheless, these limits should not be arbitrary or unnecessarily severe; freedom is a precondition for personal growth for youths as well as for adults.

FOUR WRONG ASSUMPTIONS THAT CRITICALLY INFLUENCE HOW WE THINK ABOUT VALUES AND RELIGION IN PUBLIC SCHOOLS

So much for the structure of our public elementary and secondary schools. If we are going to understand the place of values in these or any other schools, we must also understand that values are not free-floating. They are grounded in one worldview or another. Indeed, much of the conflict today over specific values and issues in education (as well as in politics) involves deeper conflicts over basic worldviews, including religious worldviews.

I would like to present four assumptions—all of which appear to me to be wrong—that exert a powerful influence on how we discuss the whole issue of values and education. I do not think we can begin to understand what is really happening in America today in connection with values and religion and their relation to education and politics unless we begin to think critically about these assumptions.

1. The first assumption is that *one can divide the world neatly into the realm of the religious and the realm of the nonreligious or secular*. In a narrow sense of the term *religious*, this is possible. It is not difficult, for instance, to distinguish between a baptismal service or a bar mitzvah as cultic practices on the one hand and the secular activities of repairing a washing machine or teaching mathematics on the other. But many theologians and some sociologists argue that in a broader sense religion is that dimension of human culture (along with metaphysics) which is concerned about questions of the meaning of life and humanity's place in the universe. In this broader sense, Marxist philosophy and other specifically secular and humanistic philosophies also

speak to questions that are religious. I do not mean by this the patronizing view that even atheists secretly believe in God. There are bona fide atheists just as there are bona fide theists. Rather, I refer to the fact that human beings live out their lives in relation to certain basic values that provide meaning and purpose to life. These values function in the life of the atheist in a way that is functionally similar to the way belief in God functions in the life of the theist.

Throughout the long sweep of American history, religion has been an extremely important dimension of our total culture. It is the framework within which most Americans have dealt with meaning and value at the deepest level. It has been intimately related to what most of our people have conceived themselves to be. It has been significantly related to the most personal dimensions of the individual's existence, to matters of ultimate freedom and decision. It has provided answers to such questions as Who am I? What is life all about? How ought I to live? How should I relate to my neighbor? What goals should I pursue in life?

If we do not want to use the words *religion* and *religious* in connection with these deeper dimensions of human existence, we might well choose terms such as *metaphysical* or *existential*. But then I would want to argue that we should extend the meaning of the First Amendment to protect a person's most deeply held secular beliefs, because, as I say, these beliefs function in the life of the agnostic or atheist very much like religious beliefs function in the life of the theist.

This is the tack the U.S. Supreme Court took in *Seeger v. United States* (1965) and in *Welsh v. United States* (1970) when it brought nontheists under the umbrella of statutory law designed to protect religious freedom of conscience. In doing this, it permitted the conscientious objector who was an agnostic or an atheist to receive exemption from regular military service—on the basis of strongly and consistently held *secular* beliefs, which, in the Court's judgment, functioned like religious beliefs. Similarly, in *Torcasso v. Watkins* (1961), the Court held as unconstitutional Maryland's requirement that public officeholders declare belief in the existence of God. In reversing the Maryland Court of Appeals decision, the justices distinguished between "those religions based on a belief in the existence of God as against those religions founded on different beliefs." In a footnote, "Secular Humanism" is cited as being one of the latter. The Court's interpretation in this case was consistent with the practice of John Dewey and other atheistic humanists who openly referred to their own secular belief systems as "religious."³

Unfortunately, the Court has tended to limit this broader interpretation of the term *religion* to the free exercise clause of the First Amendment, and it continues to work with an exceedingly narrow definition of religion when dealing with establishment cases. If the Court were to acccept the more comprehensive definition of religion in a consistent fashion, it would have to extend the meaning of the establishment clause to cover not just religion but also people's basic worldviews, their deepest metaphysical and existential commitments, their basic understandings of the meaning and goal of human existence. Extending the First Amendment in this way would indicate recognition of the truth that government has no business intruding into the most intimate dimensions of a person's life—unless a powerful state interest for doing so could be established (e.g., prohibiting racial violence on the part of people who claim a divine calling to persecute blacks, prohibiting parents from refusing blood transfusions for their children, overriding the wishes of parents who for some perverse reason want to keep their children illiterate). But then the burden of proof would lie with the state, not with the individual citizen. Government would be more adequately prevented from trying to instruct children or anyone else about the basic goals or meaning of life either explicitly or implicitly. The message would be sent that it was not to try to foster or hinder belief at this most fundamental level—belief either religious or nonreligious in the narrow sense of the term. John Stuart Mill went so far as to claim that "all attempts by the State to bias the conclusions of its citizens on disputed subjects, are evil."⁴ But this may be too strong. Although government ought not to intrude into those areas of life that have to do with people's deepest convictions and beliefs, it might be justified in trying to persuade citizens to save energy in a time of shortage or to observe speed limits on highways even if these are matters of public dispute.

At the time the First Amendment was written, the term *religion* was adequate to protect virtually all Americans from inappropriate intrusion of government into the most personal and sacred dimensions of their lives. This is no longer the case. Fairness would seem to demand that we consciously extend the meaning of the term—though in order

---

3. Dewey, *A Common Faith* (New Haven: Yale University Press, 1934), p. 87.
4. Mill, *On Liberty* (1859; rpt., New York: E. P. Dutton, 1951), p. 219.

to be fully equitable, such an extension would have to be made in First Amendment establishment cases as well as in free exercise cases.

As it stands, most First Amendment censorship rulings already recognize the incompetence of government in such matters, and they have in fact rendered what I am proposing common practice in many (but by no means all) respects. But in a larger sense, I am arguing that we should come to view the First Amendment more holistically. We should interpret the religion clauses in light of the freedom of speech, press, and assembly clauses, and we should extend all of them to refer to the domain of education.

One might object to all this, however, by arguing that government has a legitimate interest in a virtuous citizenry and that no society can long survive which does not deliberately seek to develop character and virtue in its citizens. George Will has pressed this case, and Robert Bellah and Richard Neuhaus have similarly approached the issue.[5] Within limits, self-interest may provide a sound basis for an economic system, but there is no good evidence that any society can long survive if its citizenry is not strongly committed to the greater public good. If this is so, then should not government take steps to inculcate appropriate virtues in its citizens? Is this not a legitimate, indeed a compelling, state interest? The question cannot be avoided by serious political theorists. I see at least two ways of approaching it.

On the one hand, we could continue what has been common practice in public schools since their early beginnings: we could permit or even encourage schools to teach students those basic moral values that are reflected in the founding documents of the nation and that are widely accepted by almost all Americans, whether they are religious or nonreligious in the traditional sense of these terms. Such values would include basic honesty and decency, respect for the dignity and rights of others, fairness, justice, courtesy, public-mindedness, and others. During the nineteenth and early twentieth centuries, such moral instruction typically was firmly embedded in a Protestant Christian worldview, but such is not necessary and clearly would not be appropriate today.

On the other hand, we could accept the fact that the state has an interest in establishing a virtuous citizenry but argue that it would be

---

5. See Will, *Statecraft as Soulcraft* (New York: Simon & Schuster, 1983); Bellah, *The Broken Covenant: American Civil Religion in Time of Trial* (New York: Seabury Press, 1975); and Neuhaus, *The Naked Public Square: Religion and Democracy in America* (Grand Rapids: Eerdmans, 1984).

unwise for the state to try to meet this need directly. After all, the state also has a compelling interest in the economic well-being of its citizens, but most Americans believe that it would be unwise for the state to try to meet this need directly by nationalizing all business and industry and resorting to centralized economic planning. The experiences of the Soviet Union and the Republic of China, where such approaches have been tried, have not been encouraging. The state might better use its power to lend support to those "mediating structures" that have a strong and abiding interest in civic virtue and the welfare of the entire community—such structures as religious institutions, schools, voluntary and nonprofit organizations, labor and business groups, neighborhoods, and the family, which stand between the individual and the state.[6] To be sure, such groups can lose sight of the public interest and become little more than private lobbies, a part of what Theodore Lowi calls "interest-group liberalism,"[7] but that need not inevitably be the case. When genuinely concerned about the public interest, such mediating structures provide healthy checks and balances to the power of the state. In terms of creating a virtuous citizenry, there probably is safety in such diversity; it may be a fatal mistake for the state to take on the role of inculcating or fostering virtue in its citizens. Consider the terrifying blunders and injustices of states such as Nazi Germany, the Soviet Union, and the Republic of China which have made the attempt. Tax exemptions are one means we currently use to encourage nongovernment groups to meet these public needs.

When the state tries to inculcate virtue in its citizens directly, it faces the problem that moral teachings or moral values are fully intelligible only in relationship to a larger worldview or understanding of life. How can government teach virtue in public schools—other than simply repeating certain maxims or rules—apart from relating moral values to a worldview? In part it can do this through teaching literature, but then the selection of literature becomes controversial. Which novels and plays and poems should be assigned to students? How should teachers respond when children ask why they should follow these rules or obey these moral principles? They could truthfully say that in a pluralistic society there are many possible answers to such a question, and they

---

6. For more on these "mediating structures," see Peter L. Berger and Richard John Neuhaus, *To Empower People: Mediating Structures in Public Policy* (Washington: American Enterprise Institute for Public Policy Research, 1977).

7. Lowi, *The End of Liberalism: The Second Republic of the United States*, 2d ed. (New York: W. W. Norton, 1979).

could take the time to explore the answers that various groups would give. But will this in fact happen? Will teachers take the time to point out that one reason Jews believe we should be compassionate to the alien and the foreigner is that God was compassionate to Israel when it was in the position of the stranger? Will teachers explain that Christians understand love of neighbor as a grateful response to the love they have experienced through the life, death, and resurrection of Jesus Christ? In my view the schools have become so secularized that many teachers would be unlikely to provide these sorts of anwers; indeed, I suspect that many of them would maintain that such answers violate in some way the establishment clause of the First Amendment. Most teachers, I think, would either avoid such questions altogether or else answer them entirely within a secular, nontheistic, philosophical framework.

This is also common practice at the university level. In state universities we find very few, if any, bona fide theologians doing theological ethics. When ethics are done in the modern state university—that is, when scholars actually seek out what they believe to be correct answers to specific contemporary problems—they usually work within a framework of secular philosophical ethics. In a few cases professors of religion will wrestle with current moral issues in the field of personal or social ethics, but most would consider approaching such a task *as a Lutheran* or *as a Catholic* or *as an Orthodox Jew* to be out of place in a such a context. Confessional theology or ethics is seen as belonging in the theological seminary and the denominational college, not in the state university.

In European universities it is not uncommon for confessional theologians or moralists to work side by side with secular philosophers, but in the United States such behavior is generally construed as a violation of the establishment clause of the First Amendment. And yet, as I have been contending, since secular or nontheistic philosophical ethics are not religiously neutral, the state really has no business applying this double standard, permitting nontheistic philosophers to do ethics while giving the cold shoulder to ethics taught by confessional theologians.

To say that the philosophical approach to ethics is "rational" or "based on reason" (and thus belongs in the university), whereas the theological approach is "dogmatic" and "irrational" or "nonrational," is, I think, to use these terms as ideological clubs. Both approaches rest on unprovable assumptions. Both involve faith commitments of a sort.

2. The second assumption I wish to challenge is actually an extension or an application of the first—namely, that *a secular education*

can be religiously neutral. In order to understand the power of this widely held but mistaken belief, particularly as it functions in American education, we must go back at least as far as Thomas Jefferson and his conviction that his own deistic and Enlightenment morality and religion were "nonsectarian." They were based on reason, he claimed, and they were universal. He maintained that orthodox Christians adhered to a parochial faith that was rooted in dogma and revelation, and hence they were "sectarians."

Jefferson insisted that his own nonsectarian religion and morality were worthy enough to inform the public life of the new nation but that sectarian religion—that is, the religion of all traditional Christians—should be practiced only in private, in homes and churches. He advocated religious freedom for the sectarians, but he expected them to behave themselves, to keep to themselves and to stop short of intruding their beliefs and values into the public square.

Jefferson's position is more self-serving than self-evident, however. His Enlightenment faith was just that—a *faith* commitment, a metaphysical and religious worldview that is no more obviously based on reason than are the beliefs of Christians. Both positions involve convictions that could not be derived from reason as such. They rest on basic assumptions about the nature of reality that can be described as "reasonable" but that cannot be proven by reason. They rather constitute the foundation for all subsequent reasoning.[8]

Jefferson's distinction between sectarian and nonsectarian religion has become in our own day roughly the dichotomy between the religious and the secular. Not a few moderns, like Jefferson, wrongly assume that their secular beliefs are based on scientific reason and are universal. Such individuals typically talk about means, not ends. They can tolerate religious belief so long as it is kept private and does not interfere with public policy. For many moderns it is permissible, for instance, to defend abortion on secular philosophical grounds, but it is not permissible to oppose it for reasons of faith.

To the credit of Jefferson, it must be said that he did not maintain that religion as such ought not to be a part of the public discourse—that is, he did not object to the proper, nonsectarian variety of religion.

---

8. On this, see Rockne McCarthy, Donald Oppewal, Walfred Peterson, and Gordon Spykman, *Society, State, and Schools: A Case for Structural and Confessional Pluralism* (Grand Rapids: Eerdmans, 1981); and Rockne McCarthy, James W. Skillen, and William A. Harper, *Disestablishment a Second Time: Genuine Pluralism for American Schools* (Grand Rapids: Eerdmans, 1982).

Modern secularists, with the support of such people as atheist Madelyn Murray O'Hair, People for the American Way, and the American Civil Liberties Union, on the other hand, want to clear the public square of religion altogether—failing to understand, of course, that their own views are no more religiously neutral or based on reason than the views of the Catholics and evangelicals they oppose. It is both unfair and philosophically naive to argue, as Sidney Hook has, that humanist ethics deserve to be taught in public schools because they are based on reason, whereas Christian ethics should be excluded because they are grounded in dogma and revelation.[9]

A growing number of philosophers today argue that our use of the terms "rational" and "reasonable" are culturally conditioned in a manner that is not altogether different from our use of terms such as "good" and "right." When humanists such as Hook point to the rationality of their own position and to the dogmatic quality of Christian belief, they tend to use the terms *rational* and *reasonable* as ideological weapons, making their meanings as much bound to a particular time and place as are our conceptions of the good.[10]

3 The third assumption is that *democracy and pluralism will be better served if we require a child to be exposed to a multiplicity of values rather than to only a few*. This presumably democratic procedure is, among other things, supposed to make children more tolerant of other people's points of view. Advocates of this position emphasize the importance of opening the minds of young children to new ideas and to new values. But why is such a procedure considered good? Actually, we just as often want students to make up their minds, to hold onto certain truths firmly. I do not want my students to keep an open mind about whether Paris is the capital of France rather than, say, of Italy. They have nothing to gain by doing so. Nor do I want them to be openminded about whether justice and equality are worthy goals for society. That one of these propositions is a question of fact and the other a matter of value is not crucially important, *unless* we make the prior philosophical judgment that facts can be known to be true or false but values are merely matters of opinion. In both cases I intend to teach my students the truth of these propositions and urge them to adjust their lives accordingly. Of course, it is good to keep an open mind on ques-

---

9. Hook, "Is Secular Humanism a Religion?" *The Humanist*, September/October 1976, pp. 5-7.

10. See Hilary Putnam, *Reason, Truth and History* (Cambridge: Cambridge University Press, 1981), pp. 103-200.

tions that are still open questions. But life will be far simpler and more productive for those who make up their minds about certain issues. To deliberately choose to live in bewilderment and perplexity when reasonable answers are available is no great virtue; indeed, clinging to such a choice makes a meaningful and productive life impossible.

Obviously, what constitutes open and closed questions is dependent on one's basic worldview. But inasmuch as there is no sure way to sort out one from the other to everyone's satisfaction, we will all do well not to overemphasize the certainty of our knowledge claims. And clearly we should not discourage children from asking questions or expressing doubts. If I say that the earth is round and a student responds "But it looks flat to me," I will give reasons for my statement. Likewise, if a child questions the importance of justice, tolerance, and equality, I will try to explain why these values are important to a democratic society. But I do not want the child to go away thinking that beliefs about the shape of the earth or the appropriateness of justice, tolerance, and equality are simply matters of personal preference.

The position that children should be exposed to a multiplicity of values furthermore presupposes that, for the sake of what is viewed as a good cause, the state has the right to violate parents' wishes for their children's moral and religious development. This position also precludes consideration of the very difficult psychological issue of how much exposure to a diversity of values is good for the moral development of children.

In the important 1969 case *Tinker v. Des Moines School District*, the Supreme Court, defending the students' freedom of speech, declared that "in our system, state-sponsored schools may not be enclaves of totalitarianism." Students, the court emphasized, "may not be regarded as closed-circuit recipients of only that which the state chooses to communicate."[11] But insofar as the justices did not address the question of the monopolistic nature of the school system, their analysis is misleading. For dissenting minorities, the term *only* ("only that which the state chooses to communicate") may not be of critical concern. Such minorities rather worry that many educators tend to treat students as "closed-circuit recipients" of *everything* (sex education, Values Clarification, humanistic values, etc.) "the state wishes to communicate." If so, is not this also a form of totalitarianism? As Kenneth Strike asks, "Why should the state have the right to compel parents to submit their

---

11. *Tinker v. Des Moines*, 393 U.S. 503, 506 (1969).

children to a curriculum which may lead the child to defect from the parents' values?"[12]

4. The desire to expose a child to a multiplicity of values frequently is based on the particular assumption that *ethical judgments are basically subjective* and that *we can have reliable knowledge of facts but not of values*. Since we cannot know which values are true and which are false or which are better or worse, why not expose children to many values and let them make up their own minds?

Ethical subjectivism—the position that value judgments are simply expressive of personal feelings and preferences—is widely adhered to today in academic circles, even though most professional philosophers do not accept the position. They realize that radical subjectivism paralyzes ethical discussion. Ironically, however, a great many students and faculty still hold to a subjectivist position with unquestioned allegiance. When students try to end a discussion with the comment "But that's just your value judgment," they apparently mean "Since you are just expressing your feelings—that is, your own personal opinion—your point has no general relevance for others."

Such a comment is no less strange than a statement such as "Oh, that's just your fact judgment," or "Don't press your facts on me. I have to make up my own mind whether water is made up of hydrogen and oxygen or not."

If it is indeed impossible to determine which values are better and which are worse, it may make sense to expose students to many different values in hopes that they can find some that appeal to them and that they can accept. Clearly, however, we do not want to apply this tactic in teaching chemistry or geography, for in these disciplines we believe there are right and wrong—or at least better and worse—answers.

But perhaps ethics is not as totally different from natural science and social studies as is often assumed. Both science and ethics typically start with certain basic assumptions about the nature of the world, the functioning of the human mind, and so forth. Both ways of thinking assume the law of noncontradiction and depend for their success on the prior commitment of practitioners to truth telling. Neither can make any progress at all if it starts with initial skepticism and doubt.

What constitutes knowledge in ethics is both similar to and differ-

---

12. Strike, review of *Dealing with Censorship*, ed. James E. Davis, *Harvard Educational Review* 50 (August 1980): 436.

ent from what constitutes knowledge in a natural science, but the differences are less striking than many assume them to be.

Also, it is important to remember that we can believe in the existence of objective values or even moral absolutes without at the same time insisting that we have an absolutely certain knowledge of what these values or absolutes are or of how they should be applied in every situation.

At first glance, ethical subjectivism sounds like a tolerant philosophy, appropriate for a democratic society. It dictates that no one try to tell others what is good or right for them, that each individual will have to choose on his or her own individual values. But this is misleading. To be specific, if all values are subjective, matters of personal feeling, then we can place no absolute value on such things as justice, tolerance of people who hold dissenting views, freedom and equality, or even democracy itself. Presumably, at another time or another place, people might place a higher value on injustice, tyranny, intolerance. However, most Americans believe that values rest on a surer foundation, that they are fundamentally true, that we possess certain inalienable rights quite apart from what individuals might happen to think about these issues at any given moment in history.

Many teachers and professors of education do not seem to be aware that on the metaethical level they are simply indoctrinating their students in the position that all value judgments are subjective and relative. Alan C. Purves writes confidently that a student "will respect the responses of others as being as valid for him as his is for him. He will recognize his differences from other people," but "the teacher must encourage the student to tolerate responses that differ from his."[13] And yet surely this position is open to question. In a democracy, we should teach students to be tolerant of *persons* who hold differing views, but why should students or teachers be any more tolerant of a wrong answer to a moral question—the decision to commit murder or rape, say, or advocacy of racism or treachery—than they are of wrong answers to a science or geography question.

Not only does the subjectivist position fail to supply an adequate basis for a democratic and pluralistic society, but state coercion in basic value formation as a means of furthering tolerance and democracy ought to strike us as odd at the very least. If we cannot know which val-

---

13. Purves, in *How Porcupines Make Love: Notes on a Response-Centered Curriculum*, ed. Alan C. Purves (New York: John Wiley, 1972), pp. 31, 37.

ues are worthy of assent, then we cannot know that it is good to expose the child to more rather than fewer competing values.

PUBLIC SCHOOLS AND A FREE SOCIETY

If my analysis is correct, radical change is needed in America's system of schools to ensure that freedom of conscience and freedom in teaching and learning will be fostered. It simply is not possible to preserve the First Amendment rights of various religious and ideological minorities in our current government-monopoly system. Furthermore, insofar as our public school system remains geographically exclusive and functionally private, the poor will not fare well within it.

The 1948 United Nations Universal Declaration of Human Rights states that every person has a right to free education at the "elementary and fundamental stages" and that "parents have a prior right to choose the kind of education that shall be given to their children." Obviously, America's government-monopoly school system does not incorporate that sort of emphasis on parental choice.

Although I agree that government has a powerful and legitimate interest in requiring children to be educated—I am no libertarian or anarchist—I nonetheless maintain that genuine freedom in teaching and learning will be possible only when government completely gets out of the business of actually operating schools. I see no way that the full integrity of the First Amendment can be preserved as long as government chooses to control the certification of teachers and the curricula of schools. The situation becomes intolerable when government also holds an effective monopoly in the funding of education such that some students have no realistic economic choice but to attend government schools.

For obvious reasons, however, I am not sanguine about the possibility of such a drastic change taking place any time in the near future. From a pragmatic standpoint, I would suggest that reformers ought not to concentrate on abolishing government schools but rather on disestablishing them by gradually withdrawing direct support and implementing a universal tuition voucher or entitlement system, roughly analogous to the GI bill instituted after World War II. Such a move would allow for genuine pluralism and diversity of values. Parents who were dissatisfied with the curricula of government schools could afford to enroll their children elsewhere. They would no longer need to play the role of the critic and the protester or, from the perspective of many within the public school establishment, the censor.

Another possibility would be to provide funds directly to private schools, both religious and secular. This pattern is used in Canada, Israel, and a variety of European nations, but in the United States it is unlikely that it would be seen by the courts as compatible with the establishment clause of the First Amendment.

In a voucher system, government (local and/or state, with possible federal assistance) would provide tuition vouchers that parents could redeem for their children's education at schools of the parents' choice. Both government and nongovernment schools could accept vouchers. Ideally, the dollar value of vouchers would be inversely related to family income levels (to permit poor families to bid for high-quality education), and adjustments would be made for local cost-of-living differences and for varying costs of vocational and academic curricula. Appropriate prohibitions against discrimination on the basis of race and national origin would also be built into the system.

Vouchers would probably create healthy competition for both government and nongovernment schools and thus lead to greater efficiency, but their prime justification would be related to freedom of conscience. Parents would no longer be forced to send their children to schools whose values and practices offended or even violated their deepest religious beliefs and moral convictions. Some parents believe that the present school system is far too competitive; or that it emphasizes science and math too much and music, art, and literature too little; or that it does not sufficiently stress environmental values. Vouchers would for the first time permit these parents to exercise genuine choice in their children's education.

Clearly vouchers could create problems of their own. Racist parents might attempt to manipulate the system to resegregate schools. Some have speculated that a voucher system could result in the least capable students being abandoned (the term *warehoused* has been used) in the public schools. In these areas (and other areas in which problems might arise) voucher supporters would have to give assurances of their commitment to equality, justice, and nonracist policies.

But the problems with a voucher system remain a matter of speculation; the problems associated with the coercive nature of our public school monopoly, on the other hand, are a present reality for dissenting minorities. Stephen Arons goes so far as to argue that "the present political and financial structure of American schooling is unconstitutional."[14] At the very least it presents a disturbing problem for many

---

14. Arons, *Compelling Belief*, p. 198.

parents today. If government can control the enculturation and basic value formation of children during ten to thirteen years of schooling, then how can the First Amendment's guarantee of freedom of speech and religion be a fully meaningful concept?

Even if government schools are disestablished through the implementation of a universal voucher system, the government schools that survive disestablishment—precisely because they are public and not private—must become more genuinely pluralist in curriculum, structure, and goals. Rather than trying to rid the schools of all religion and thus in effect giving a state-sponsored advantage to secular and humanistic beliefs and values, government schools that survive disestablishment should permit various values, worldviews, and religious beliefs to exist side by side. In such circumstances, widespread accommodation and compromise would be essential. Christian and Jewish beliefs and values should be substantially represented in the curriculum. In line with the Equal Access legislation signed into law during the summer of 1984 by President Reagan, Christian, Jewish, and Islamic clubs as well as secular and humanistic groups would be permitted in the schools as extracurricular activities. The school day and perhaps some classes might begin with a moment of silence during which students would be free to pray or not to pray as each individual would choose. Religious symbols would not be totally excluded from public school buildings under the false assumption of the religious neutrality of the secular. It would be essential for the schools to teach and practice tolerance even of those people who hold unpopular views, and they would have to show a willingness to live with compromises that might well be complex. Overall, such a scheme would better do justice to the spirit of the First Amendment than do the largely secular and humanistic curricula and practices of present-day public schools.

Insofar as the courts and groups such as the American Civil Liberties Union and People for the American Way have failed to realize the inescapably religious nature of education, their activities have been largely misdirected and, in my judgment, have tended to undermine the very First Amendment freedoms they are ostensibly fighting to preserve. Indeed, most moderns tend to view education largely within the context of bureaucracy, efficiency, and value neutrality rather than as a deeply personal, spiritual, and religious matter, an experience that demands freedom of a radical sort. That public education aspires to value neutrality, a focus on the "facts," and a rejection of a specifically Christian worldview, however, does not mean that it can escape making its own value judgments and committing itself to an alternative worldview.

It is not possible simply to focus on the "facts," for as philosophers of science have stressed in recent years, all observation is "theory-laden." What we count as a "fact" is very much dependent on our particular worldview.

TWO FINAL QUESTIONS

Two important questions remain unanswered.

1. *Will responsibility and authority for the education of children (including the inculcation of beliefs and values) rest primarily with the parents or with the state?* Americans have traditionally assumed that this responsibility should be placed on the parents. Public schools have been understood to function in loco parentis, but recent trends suggest that the state is expanding its power over children at an increasing rate.

Admittedly, almost all Americans believe that the freedom of parents to make decisions about their children's education should not be viewed as absolute. Children need to be protected from parental negligence and abuse, and the state has a compelling interest in making sure that its citizens become economically competent to function in a modern technological society (so that they will not become wards of the state dependent on public welfare) as well as sufficiently knowledgeable to become effective citizens in a democratic society. These state needs could be met in a voucher system by establishing minimum standards for instruction in such basic subject areas as reading, writing, mathematics, and civics as a requirement for eligibility to receive vouchers.

Already in the initial establishment of government-operated schools in the first half of the nineteenth century, however, the state expanded its power over children beyond what might be defined as compelling state interest. And with the increasing centralization of power in government schools—power to choose textbooks, determine curriculum, and set standards—the idea of local control of public schools and of the schools functioning in loco parentis has become a comforting but grossly inaccurate myth.

To be sure, if parents are given more control over the education of their children, they will make mistakes, and some of them might be harmful. But giving excessive power to the state constitutes a far greater risk—namely, the risk of tyranny, state indoctrination, loss of freedom, and destruction of genuine pluralism.

We have already noted the emphasis in the United Nations Universal Declaration of Human Rights on parental involvement in choosing the kind of education their children should have. The Second

Vatican Council used similar language when addressing the question of educational freedom, suggesting that civil authorities should see to it that children can be educated "according to the moral and religious convictions of each family." Also, when choosing schools for their children, parents should be "genuinely free to follow their consciences." Thus civil authorities should make sure that no school monopoly develops, "for such a monopoly would militate against the native rights of the human person, the development and spread of culture itself, the peaceful association of citizens, and the pluralism which exists today in very many societies."[15]

Considering the fundamental importance of true family choice in education, it may be that Christians and others concerned about the survival of genuine pluralism should seek a constitutional amendment that would formalize the kind of educational rights mentioned by these two important documents.

If the state's monopoly in education were to be broken by disestablishing public schools and turning to a system of universal education tuition vouchers, parents would be free to choose for their children the education they consider most appropriate for preserving the religious or secular beliefs and values of the family. This would not entail their doing the actual teaching—in most cases that is best left in the hands of professional educators—but they should keep control of the process. Nor would it prevent professional educators from exercising their own judgment or practicing their special skills. Sensitive parents should recognize that teachers are professionals and that no good will come from interfering too much in the teaching process. Under the voucher system, parents would be exercising their control by taking care to choose schools that would reinforce values and generally be capable of meeting the particular needs of their children; beyond that, they would in effect be entrusting their children to the teachers, administrators, and others who made up the staff of those schools.

Contracts between parents and schools could be made in an atmosphere of freedom, for power would no longer reside mainly in the hands of the state and of the school as a representative of the state.

Many educators seem to assume that if we were to grant parents more freedom to choose the kind of education their children should have, too many would want to impart to their children a narrow, bigoted, intolerant worldview. But that is to indict the parents as

---

15. *The Documents of Vatican II*, ed. Walter M. Abbott (New York: Herder & Herder, 1966), pp. 645, 644.

incompetent, bigoted, and narrow-minded on very little evidence, to hold them guilty till proven innocent. Actually, as Charles Glenn points out, from the very beginning of the drive for government public schools, Horace Mann and other proponents of public education were intent on reforming society by changing the values of children. Mann had little sympathy for Calvinists or Catholics, and he was determined to use every legal means—including state coercion in schooling—to ensure that other people's children were taught the truth as he understood it.

Many contemporary public school educators still seem to think that they have the truth and that it is incumbent on them to make sure that this truth gets passed on to children. They believe that it would simply be too dangerous to permit parents—especially poor parents—to be able to choose the kind of education they wanted for their children.

Is it not curious that so many liberal educators believe that the salvation of the world is to be found in education and that it is professional educators—that is, themselves—who should determine the content of education? And yet at the same time these experts accept the use of state coercion to ensure that pupils attend the government-monopoly schools that they support, regularly opposing the kind of freedom of choice that tuition vouchers would permit.

Just as in an earlier age Americans decided against the establishment of a single national church by the federal government (a principle later extended to the individual states), so today we can decide to relinquish our system of government-established schools in favor of educational freedom. The need for such a move becomes increasingly acute as local control of public schools gives way to centralized bureaucratic government control and to control by the courts.

2. *How much freedom are the political majority and those in power willing to give to dissenting minorities, to people who hold points of view different from those of the majority?* Are we as a nation really committed to pluralism, to the preservation of differences, or do we believe that government—acting on behalf of the political majority and through the bureaucratic structures of the educational establishment—knows best how to educate and socialize children? Do we adequately appreciate the role of *structural* pluralism? Liberal educators often tend to see pluralism in terms of the individual student's right to free expression and freedom to read and learn what he or she wants. But surely this is naive. Pluralism will almost certainly become meaningless if it is no more than a matter of individuals making isolated value choices. If we have learned anything from sociology, it is that values are related to

communities and that traditions depend on enabling structures to survive and flourish.

One argument made against educational vouchers is that such a system would lead to excessive fragmentation of society. Everyone would do his or her own thing. People would likely commit themselves to all sorts of strange goals and values and society would not be able to hold together. Significantly, this is roughly the same argument that was pressed over two hundred years ago in defense of a federally established church in America. Society would fall apart and become a collection of contentious fragments without such an ecclesial structure to bind it together, it was argued. People would be taught and would commit themselves to all sorts of strange beliefs. Yet we know that this did not happen. On the contrary, the establishment prohibition has led to a great freedom and creativity in American culture. We have become a truly open society, at least in comparison to most nations of the world.

Of course, one reason why the absence of a national church has not led to social fragmentation is precisely that government schools gradually came to provide the social glue that in earlier forms of society was provided by a common religious frame. One of the chief motivations for establishing a system of government schools was to counter what was felt to be the pernicious and potentially divisive influence of the large numbers of Roman Catholic immigrants entering the United States during the first part of the nineteenth century. Public schools were meant to teach these immigrants correct values and initiate them into the American way.

Curiously, many political liberals who today support a system of government schools to ensure some sort of social cohesion also favor bilingual education for Hispanics and others. And many conservatives who are open to or in favor of disestablishment and educational vouchers oppose bilingual school programs. Some would say this suggests that the critical issue is not that of social fragmentation per se but rather whether the state can be genuinely neutral about religion in government schools. Liberals by and large think it can and thus dismiss Catholic and fundamentalist criticisms of public schools as misguided, as an outgrowth of right-wing political commitments. In the end, however, the evidence is stronger that both school supporters and school critics are, for the most part, concerned about potential social fragmentation.

Those who support a system of education that is under majoritarian control need to ask themselves whether their commitment to such control is principled or opportunistic. Would their commitment to such majoritarian control remain firm, for instance, if the Moral Majority truly became a majority and were able to dominate the hiring of teachers, the choice of curriculum, and the process of book selection in the schools? And what if at the same time we had a Supreme Court that looked favorably on the social philosophy of this new majority? Under such circumstances those who presently are strongly opposed to family choice in education and to tuition vouchers might have serious second thoughts about their position.

Are we Americans willing to let people think for themselves; to preserve their particular religious, social, and moral traditions; and to take charge of the education of their own children? Distressingly, many educators seem more intent on improving and reforming society by controlling the schooling of other people's children than they seem to be committed to basic freedom of speech and basic freedom in teaching and learning.[16] The same people who criticize the Fundamentalists for being censors and bookburners and who speak a great deal about academic freedom appear to be unwilling to let other people take charge of their own education and the education of their children. They want to maintain majority control of the schools even if dissenting minorities find such control coercive and oppressive. Their concern that racism would increase or that society would become too fragmented under a voucher system must be taken seriously, but at the same time it must not be allowed to become a rationalization for their continued control of the public schools. But of course voucher advocates must be sure that their own motives are honorable too. Establishing a voucher system as a means of guaranteeing freedom of conscience and preserving genuine pluralism is defensible; attempting to preserve economically and racially segregated schools is not.

Education can be viewed primarily as a means of imparting technical skills to children that will enable them to function effectively in a technological, control-oriented society. It can be seen as an opportunity to reform society by influencing children. But it can also be understood mainly in terms of the freedom of the human spirit, in connection with the rights of people of diverse traditions to survive and flourish, and in light of America's historic commitments to religious liberty and freedom of conscience.

Genuine pluralism in education will demand great tolerance for diversity, and, to use Victor Ferkiss's apt expression, a willingness to avoid showing too much "impatience with the messiness of ordinary

---

16. On this, see Charles Glenn's "Molding Citizens," pp. 25-56 herein.

human life," an impatience he takes to be "the real mark of the true totalitarian."[17] Most Americans have come to understand that nineteenth- and twentieth-century public schools, dominated as they were by Protestant Christian values and beliefs, were oppressive to Jews and atheists and even to Roman Catholic Christians. But today we should not make the opposite mistake of supporting a monopolistic government school system that gives a state-sponsored advantage to secular and humanistic values. Neither justice nor cultural or religious diversity will be well served by continuing to support such a system. Indeed, support will simply serve to turn the secular into a new form of sectarianism and to hinder powerfully liberating features of the American political experiment.

---

17. Ferkiss, *Technological Man: The Myth and the Reality* (New York: New American Library, 1969), pp. 88-89.

"Molding" Citizens

Charles L. Glenn

My texts for this meditation are both taken from the Constitution of the Commonwealth of Massachusetts. The first is Chapter V, Section II of the original document, drafted by John Adams in 1779, ratified in June 1780:

> Wisdom, and knowledge, as well as virtue, diffused generally among the body of the people, being necessary for the preservation of their rights and liberties; and as these depend on spreading the opportunities and advantages of education in the various parts of the country, and among the different orders of the people, it shall be the duty of Legislatures and Magistrates, in all future periods of this Commonwealth, to cherish the interests of literature and the sciences, and all seminaries of them; especially the university at Cambridge, public schools and grammar schools in the towns; to encourage private societies and public institutions, rewards and immunities, for the promotion of agriculture, arts, sciences, commerce, trades, manufactures, and a natural history of the country; to countenance and inculcate the principles of humanity and general benevolence, public and private charity, industry and frugality, honesty and punctuality in their dealings; sincerity, good humour, and all social affections, and generous sentiments among the people.

The second is an excerpt from Article XVIII of the Amendments, ratified in 1855 (it has been modified several times since in the interest of greater specificity):

All moneys raised by taxation in the towns and cities for the support of public schools, and all moneys which may be appropriated by the State for the support of common schools, shall be applied to, and expended in, no other schools than those which are conducted according to law, under the order and superintendence of the authorities of the town or city in which the money is to be expended; and such moneys shall never be appropriated to any religious sect for the maintenance exclusively of its own schools.

In the first three-quarters of a century of our national history much had changed. The original Massachusetts Constitution breathes a spirit of optimism about the beneficent role of schools and other institutions of popular enlightenment, while the amendment of 1855 was one expression of a reaction against the growing Irish Catholic population of Boston and other cities, which included an almost total "Know-Nothing" (anti-immigrant) sweep of elections to the legislature in 1854. The earlier language, as Rockne McCarthy would want me to point out, takes for granted that government would patronize and cooperate with a variety of agencies for promoting public virtue, including many we would now consider private or "sectarian." The language approved by the voters in 1855 draws a sharp line between those schools under the direct control of elected officials and all other schools.

My concern is not with this discontinuity, however, nor with the vexed question of public funding for nonpublic schooling, but with the common assumptions that underlie the two texts. These are assumptions about why government should be concerned about education, and they are as much present in the generous language of 1780 as they are in the mean language of 1855. They continue to confuse our thinking about appropriate policy toward education today.

I. EARLY VIEWS OF THE PURPOSES OF REPUBLICAN EDUCATION

The concern of John Adams and the other drafters in 1780 was primarily with what today is the unfashionable area of "character education." In this they stood in an Enlightenment tradition, which urged that the State promote popular education in order to create a moral and rational citizenry and to lessen the power of the competing loyalties to church, to region, to dialect, to occupational guild, or to local potentates.

In discussing the development of this agenda for state-directed education, it is useful to borrow a distinction from the debates over education policy that took place during the French Revolution. "Instruction," in these debates, meant the teaching of the basic and advanced skills useful to economic life, while "education" meant the development of attitudes, loyalties, and values. Schooling at virtually all times and places has included both of these objectives, in a varying mix; even post-secondary vocational programs, for example, lay stress on inculcating attitudes toward work as well as work-related skills.

Popular (elementary) schooling in Massachusetts in the years following the Revolution, as in colonial times, was provided by an assortment of local arrangements that do not fit into our present categories of "public" and "private" education. The schoolmaster might have been hired by a town or district committee of citizens, or might have set up school on his or her own initiative, especially in the larger communities. In either case, the schools were largely supported by the fees paid by parents, though various arrangements were made to pay the fees of the children of families for whom this would have been a burden. The clergy frequently took a leading role in sponsoring and overseeing schools, and religious instruction and devotions were a normal part of the school program.

The educational reformers of the 1830s and subsequent decades derided this congeries of arrangements for schooling as hopelessly inadequate, but recent research suggests that it was rather effective in assuring nearly universal literacy and basic mathematical skills as well as in preparing those students whose social status or natural ability made secondary education possible for such further study. It was effective, that is, in providing the *instruction* necessary for the farmers, craftsmen, and small tradesmen of the day and in laying a basis for further study for those who were in a position to go on.

The "common school revival" that began in the late 1820s and received definitive form under the leadership of Horace Mann was a struggle over *education* as opposed to *instruction*, over the role of schools in shaping the character of the American people. My purposes here are to demonstrate this proposition and to show how Mann and others set about creating a system of popular education in the interest of their convictions about the necessary direction of American life. In so doing they were setting out to realize, a half-century later, the Enlightenment program that John Adams had written into the Massachusetts Constitution.

The improvement of *instruction* was a part of the reform movements of this era of benevolent activity and was initially promoted in much the same manner as the other reforms and efforts to improve society that gained broad support about the same time, as a matter for voluntary associations, "networking," and initiatives by local elites.

Within a few years, however, the emphasis shifted from improving the techniques and resources available within multiform arrangements for schooling to state action in the interest of a uniform system of *education*. Voluntary efforts lost credit. Local diversity was defined as a problem, and schools not accountable to the political process were condemned as a threat to the best interests of society. The goal became a transformation of popular schooling into a powerful instrument for social unity.

In Massachusetts the "common school revival" was essentially an effort by a Unitarian/Whig minority—the "new class" of the day—to reshape popular beliefs and values after a single pattern. State action was necessary, in this minority's view, primarily to overcome the undesirable diversity of teaching associated with the education of many children—from poor as well as prosperous families—provided by various private and church-connected schools. This diversity was seen as harmful to progress, to social and national unity, and to the goals of the liberal elite. Particular concern was expressed about the perpetuation of religious fanaticism in schools where, as Mann observed in his *First Report* (February 1838), "children are taught from their tenderest years to wield the sword of polemics with fatal dexterity." It was hoped that the common school could, by inculcating "the beautiful and sublime truths of ethics and natural religion," protect the rising generation from falling into the "opposite extremes" of becoming "devotees on the one side or profligates on the other."

Although the common school revival took place in the era of "Jacksonian democracy," efforts by some historians to relate it to popular demands have been less than convincing; indeed, Horace Mann conceded privately that his program would never be carried out if he waited for public support. In an uncharacteristic moment of humor, he suggested that sheriffs might disperse crowds not by reading the riot act but by announcing a convention on education.

During the three decades before the Civil War, two significant developments occurred in popular education in the United States: the foundations were laid for effective state control, and the historic role of schools in transmitting religious traditions was attenuated into perfunctory observances and moralizing.

A generation earlier the exciting debates on education in the French National Assembly had awakened echoes in Jeffersonian circles in the United States, and the Enlightenment program for popular schooling was spelled out without the caution that Mann and his allies would find it necessary to employ when they actually began to implement the program.

Jefferson himself called schools the most important instrument of society for "ameliorating the condition, promoting the virtue, and advancing the happiness of man,"[1] while Benjamin Rush wrote (in 1786) that "Our schools of learning, by producing one general and uniform system of education, will render the mass of the people more homogeneous and thereby fit them more easily for uniform and peaceable government." Thus, by a sort of perpetual-motion process, popular education would produce the millennium in the new nation:

> From the combined and reciprocal influence of religion, liberty, and learning upon the morals, manners, and knowledge of individuals, of these upon government, and of government upon individuals, it is impossible to measure the degrees of happiness and perfection to which mankind may be raised. For my part, I can form no ideas of the golden age, so much celebrated by the poets, more delightful than the contemplation of that happiness which it is now in the power of the legislature of Pennsylvania to confer upon her citizens by establishing proper modes and places of education in every part of the state.[2]

This is precisely the hope that a few years later would inspire the Jacobin education reformers in the National Convention in France. Thus, for example, Napoleon's future chief of police, Fouchè, told the Convention in 1793 that

> Si nos ècoles s'organisent promptement et selon nos veux, la plus heureuse rèvolution est consommèe; tous nos succés tiennent a ce succés; il renferme toutes nos espèrances et toutes nos craintes; aucune considèration ne doit pas balancer un intèret aussi puissant.... Le peuple francais ne veut pas plus une demi-instruction qu'une demi-libertè; il veut etre règenèrè tout entier, comme un nouvel etre rècemment sorti des mains de la nature.[3]

---

1. Jefferson, quoted by Russel Blaine Nye in *The Cultural Life of the New Nation: 1776-1830* (New York: Harper Torchbooks, 1963), p. 150.
2. Rush, "A Plan for the Establishment of Public Schools and the Diffusion of Knowledge in Pennsylvania...," in *Essays on Education in the Early Republic*, ed. Frederick Rudolph (Cambridge: Belknap Press, 1965), pp 17-18, 22.
3. "If our schools are organized promptly and as we wish, the most glorious revolution will be achieved; every success depends upon that success: it bears all our hopes and all our fears; no other consideration may be set in the balance against such a powerful interest.... The French people no more want

In their confidence that popular education could completely transform the entire population, could create them anew as though they had no past and no stubborn attachment to beliefs, loyalties, and habits, Fouchè and his fellow Jacobins reflected one of the dearest convictions of the Enlightenment. By putting such a transformation forward as a popular demand, they were articulating a desire of which we may be sure the French people to whom they attributed it were unaware. As would be shown by what followed—the dismal failure of attempts to implement the radical education program in France, despite all the threats and formidable organizing energy of the Republic—the common people were determined *not* to be reshaped according to the new "republican" model.

Like the Jacobins, Rush had absorbed the Enlightenment conviction that the state should seek to refashion its people by a popular education concerned more with civic virtue and national loyalty than with literacy and other skills. The impulse to seek to mold the future through molding the children of the common people was almost irresistible to this generation of liberal idealists.

> The *present time* is peculiarly favorable to the establishment of these benevolent and necessary institutions in Pennsylvania. The minds of our people have not as yet lost the yielding texture they acquired by the heat of the late Revolution. They will *now* receive more readily than five or even three years hence new impressions and habits of all kinds.[4]

The essential ruthlessness of this ambition—caught no doubt from Rousseau—comes across in Rush's statement that

> I consider it as possible to convert men into republican machines. This must be done if we expect them to perform their parts properly in the great machine of the government of the state. That republic is sophisticated with monarchy or aristocracy that does not revolve upon the wills of the people, and these must be fitted to each other by means of education before they can be made to

---

a half-schooling than they want a half-liberty; they want to be entirely remade, like a new creature coming freshly out of the hands of Nature." Taken from *Procés*-Verbaux du Comitè d'Instruction Publique de la Convention Nationale, vol. 1, ed. M. J. Guillaume (Paris: Imprimèrie nationale, 1891), p. 616.

4. Rush, in *Essays on Education*, p. 22. See also Lawrence A. Cremin, *American Education: The National Experience, 1783-1876* (New York: Harper & Row, 1980), pp. 116-21.

produce regularity and unison in government.⁵

In 1797 the American Philosophical Society of Philadelphia awarded its prize for the best essay on "a national system of education" to Samuel Harrison Smith, editor of the Jeffersonian organ *The National Intelligencer*. Smith did not mince his words: "It is the duty of a nation to superintend and even to coerce the education of children and . . . high considerations of expediency not only justify but dictate the establishment of a system which shall place under a control, independent of and superior to parental authority, the education of children." To this end, it should be "made punishable by law in a parent to neglect offering his child to the preceptor for instruction." "Society must establish the right to educate, and acknowledge the duty of having educated, all children. A circumstance so momentously important must not be left to the negligence of individuals."⁶

This echoes the insistence of the Jacobins on the right of the state to educate all of the children of the nation in common schools—not only to overcome possible neglect by indifferent parents but also to counter the views of the parents if necessary. This Citizen Le Clerc proposed as the first article of the education statutes, "Nul ne sera dispensè d'envoyer ses enfants aux *ècoles du citoyen*." By this means,

> Au moyen de l'instruction commune, vous dèjouez le coeur des enfants a l'aristocratie des parents, a leur orgeuil, a leur fanatisme. . . . n'est-ce pas blesser l'autoritè paternelle? Non. C'est seulement exercer cella de la patrie.⁷

With respect to the content of such instruction, Smith argued that it must give primacy to the development of that "virtue" essential to the civil order and of the "wisdom" necessary to the exercise of virtue. Assuming that the purpose of education is essentially civic and secular, he proposed that it should limit itself to

> the admission into the young mind of such ideas only as are either absolutely true or in the highest degree probable. . . . Should it not be thought treason against truth and virtue to instill prejudice

---

5. Rush, in *Essays on Education*, pp. 17-18.
6. Smith, in *Essays on Education*, pp. 210, 190.
7. "No one will be excused from sending his children to the schools of citizenship. . . . By means of common instruction, you will set the hearts of the children free from the aristocratic ideas of their parents, from their pride, from their fanaticism. . . . Does that offend against the authority of parents? No. It simply exercises that of the fatherland." Taken from *Procès-Verbaux*, pp. 196-97.

and error into the young mind? . . . What shall we say of those who inculcate principles which they know to be false and attempt in this way to establish systems that only exist in the midst of human carnage and destruction? . . . Let then those truths in which all men agree be firmly impressed, let those which are probable be inculcated with caution, and let doubt always hang over those respecting which the good and the wise disagree. Above all things let the infant mind be protected from conviction without proof.[8]

Thus, "the most solemn attention must be paid to avoid instilling into the young mind any ideas or sentiments whose truth is not unequivocally established by the undissenting suffrage of the enlightened and virtuous part of mankind."

Here is a full load of Enlightenment themes, familiar from Diderot, Condorcet, and others who discussed systems of national popular education: (1) that much of orthodox religion is untrue and that those who teach its doctrines are self-serving hypocrites who know that it is untrue (by the 1830s the accusation had changed, both in Europe and the United States: they were "twisted fanatics"); (2) that religious systems have produced only "carnage and destruction"; and (3) that "the enlightened and virtuous" basically agree on both truth and morality, and thus there is a basis for a common teaching that can be entirely uplifting and that could not offend any right-thinking parent.

Since education would be compulsory, the resistance of those parents who clung to beliefs with which the enlightened and virtuous do not agree could be dismissed. Note, however, that the need for compulsory education is a tacit admission that there will not be universal agreement on this program. Horace Mann did not initially call for compulsory education, trusting in his powers of persuasion and in the growing enlightenment of the age. But eventually he did experience resistance, and it brought him finally to the conviction that the move would have to be made. Massachusetts adopted the first compulsory-attendance law in the country, in 1852.

Smith adumbrated several other themes of the later program of public education, again under direct influence of the proposals then current in France. One was the need for the development of schoolbooks that would reflect the new objectives and premises of education from a national perspective. Such works "explaining and enforcing plain and undeniable truths and avoiding prejudices or falsehoods"

---

8. Smith, in *Essays on Education*, pp. 170, 192-93, 211.

were not available, but he believed that by "offering large rewards for books of this nature" (as had become the practice of the French revolutionary government) it would be possible to develop a set of "approved books" that would render education independent of the inadequacies of teachers.

> The indispensable economy of arrangements which are to pervade a whole society will prohibit the employment of preceptors of either great or original talents. It will therefore be fit that the preceptor, instead of inculcating his own immature ideas, should be guided by prescribed works.[9]

Presumably Smith had in mind the development of American equivalents of the *Principes de la morale rèpublicaine*, the *Catèchisme rèpublicain*, the *Epitres et èvangiles du rèpublicain*, and other works developed several years before at the invitation of the National Convention in France.

Samuel Knox, who shared the essay prize with Smith, shared with him also an approval of the recent efforts to create a national education system in the service of the French Revolution.

> What has lately been done in France excepted, I know of no plan devised by individuals or attempted by any commonwealth in modern times that effectually tends to the establishment of any uniform, regular system of national education. . . . The good effects of such a system are almost self-evident. . . . Diversity of modes of education also tend not only to confound and obstruct its operation and improvement but also give occasion to many other inconveniences and disagreeable consequences that commonly arise in the various departments of civil society. . . . But were an approved system of national education to be established, all these imperfections of its present state would, in a great measure, be remedied and at the same time accompanied with many peculiar advantages hitherto unexperienced in the instruction and improvement of the human mind.[10]

This rage for a "rational" uniformity, this conviction that national education is the key to an actual progress in the human race, echoes the debates in the French National Convention.

Another note that is more peculiarly American and that would gain increasing importance in the future was a concern to create a national unity out of the diverse population of the United States through

---

9. Smith, in *Essays on Education*, p. 94.
10. Knox, in *Essays on Education*, pp. 309-10.

an educational system deliberately geared to assimilation. Knox argued that this was essential for "such a wide extent of territory inhabited by citizens blending together almost all the various manners and customs of every country of Europe. Nothing, then, surely, might be supposed to have a better effect toward harmonizing the whole in these important views than an *uniform system of national education*."[11]

This required, as Smith had insisted, an exclusion of revealed religion, which he believed would produce nothing but further divisions, from the educational process. In characteristic Jeffersonian terms Knox announced that

> It is a happy circumstance peculiarly favorable to an uniform plan of public education that this country hath excluded ecclesiastical from civil policy and emancipated the human mind from the tyranny of church authority and church establishments. It is a consequence of this principle of our happy civil constitution that theology, so far as the study of it is connected with particular forms of faith, ought to be excluded from a liberal system of national instruction, especially where there exist so many various denominations among the professors of the Christian religion.

Not that religion itself, in an extremely general sense, would be excluded. The school day should begin and end "with a short and suitable prayer and address to the great source of all knowledge and instruction."

> It might, also, be highly advantageous to youth, and in no respect interfere with the different religious sentiments of the community, to make use of a well-digested, concise moral catechism. In the first part of this catechism should be inculcated natural theology or the proofs of the existence of the Deity from his works.... The second part might properly consist of the first principles of ethics, the nature and consequence of virtue and vice, and also a concise view of economics and the relative virtues. The third and last part should inculcate, concisely, the principles of jurisprudence; the nature of civil government....[12]

The significance of the views and proposals expressed by Smith and Knox is not in their immediate impact, for they had almost none, but in the insight that they give into thinking about education in Jeffersonian circles at an early stage in the development of national institutions. The fact that the American Philosophical Society offered a

---

11. Knox, in *Essays on Education*, p. 311.
12. Knox, in *Essays on Education*, pp. 315, 332-33.

prize for the best essay on a national system of education, and selected these, makes it clear that the "radical" educational agenda of the French Revolution, derived in turn from the *philosophes*, was familiar to and even supported by some of the elite of the new nation. The complete rejection of these proposals, the lack of *any* contemporary action by Congress to create national uniformity and federal leadership in education, reflect a very different view among Americans about how education should be controlled and by whom its objectives should be set.

For all their interest in the history of the Common School Revival, we do not find Mann or other reformers of the 1830s and 1840s citing Knox or Smith in support of their very similar proposals—including an active role for the state, a board of education, regular reports on the performance of local schools, adoption of standardized school texts, religious instruction without teaching distinctively Christian doctrines, and compulsory education as an assertion of society's prior claim to children, whatever the views and desires of their parents. It was only as this program of the French Revolution was mediated through the examples of Prussia and the Netherlands and through the liberal Protestantism of New England that it became acceptable as a statement of public purpose.

II. CONTROVERSY OVER STATE LEADERSHIP IN EDUCATION

One of the better-known episodes in the history of American education is the attempt in 1840, by a substantial party within the Massachusetts legislature, to abolish Horace Mann's board of education (established in 1837) and thus his position as its secretary.

As Carl A. Kaestle and Maris A. Vinovskis have shown in a careful study,[13] it was largely the Democrats in the legislature and not the religiously orthodox as such who moved to abolish the board. This corrects the view put forward by Mann himself and repeated by most historians that the school reforms were opposed on grounds of religious obscurantism if not bigotry. Mann wrote in his diary a few months later that "the bigots and vandals had been signally defeated in their wicked attempts to destroy the Board of Education," but in fact, as Kaestle and Vinovskis show, "representatives from towns whose schools used Bibles or whose school committees included members of the clergy were less

---

13. Kaestle and Vinovskis, *Education and Social Change in Mid-Nineteenth Century Massachusetts* (Boston: Beacon Press, 1980).

hostile to the board of education than legislators from communities whose schools did not use Bibles or did not have ministers on their school boards." The finding is significant because, as they observe, "Horace Mann and the Whigs never fully appreciated the depth of the fears of the Democrats that the creation of a state agency to do good might eventually result in a serious danger to freedom within the Republic."[14] The conflicts that were to follow cannot be understood apart from the inability on the part of Mann and his allies to recognize that their opponents were neither insincere nor unenlightened, that they simply had a different view of the best interests of the emerging American democracy.

A special legislative committee had been appointed to consider how to reduce state expenditure, and it reported that the board was an unnecessary expense and a threat to political and religious freedom.

> District schools, in a republican government, need no police regulations, no system of state censorship, no checks of moral, religious, or political conservatism, to preserve either the morals, the religion, or the politics of the state. . . . Instead of consolidating the education interest of the Commonwealth in one grand central head, and that head the government, let us rather hold on to the good old principles of our ancestors, and diffuse and scatter this interest far and wide, divided and subdivided, not only into towns and districts but even into families and individuals. The moment this interest is surrendered to the government, and all responsibility is thrown upon civil power, farewell to the usefulness of common schools, the just pride, honor, and ornament of New England; farewell to religious liberty, for there would be but one church; farewell to political freedom, for nothing but the name of a republic would survive such a catastrophe.[15]

The vote to abolish Mann's position as secretary of the board failed narrowly, on a vote along strongly partisan lines.

Meanwhile, the usefulness of the board of education was studied by the Committee on Education. A majority report called for its abolition, while a minority supported the board. The report of the committee majority, recommending that the board be abolished, argued that

> since our system of public schools did not owe its origin to the

---

14. Kaestle and Vinovskis, *Education and Social Change*, pp. 214, 231.
15. Report of the special legislative committee, quoted by Kaestle and Vinovskis in *Education and Social Change*, pp. 215-16.

Board of Education, but was in existence for two centuries before that board was established, a proposal to dispense with its further services cannot be reasonably considered as indicating any feelings of hostility or of indifference towards our system of Common Schools. . . . The operations of that Board are incompatible with those principles upon which our Common Schools have been founded and maintained.[16]

The primary concern of the majority was with the potential for an inappropriate concentration in the state of the responsibility and the initiative for defining the objectives of education and thus of the character and convictions of the rising generation. The influence of the Prussian model and the more remote French example (which was not acknowledged by the education reformers themselves) was identified with sophistication and accuracy:

> After all that has been said about the French and Prussian systems, they appear to your Committee to be much more admirable, as a means of political influence, and of strengthening the hands of the government, than as a mere means for the diffusion of knowledge. For the latter purpose, the system of public Common Schools, under the control of persons most interested in their flourishing condition, who pay taxes to support them, appears to your Committee much superior. The establishment of the Board of Education seems to be the commencement of a system of centralization and of monopoly of power in a few hands, contrary, in every respect, to the true spirit of our democratical institutions; and which, unless speedily checked, may lead to unlooked-for and dangerous results.

This concern led, in turn, to the further problem of religious and moral teaching in a society that was already pluralistic.

> Your Committee has already stated, that the French and Prussian system of public schools appears to have been devised, more for the purpose of modifying the sentiments and opinions of the rising generation, according to a certain government standard, than as a mere means of diffusing elementary knowledge. Undoubtedly, Common Schools may be used as a potent means of engrafting into the minds of children, political, religious, and moral opinions;—but, in a country like this, where such diversity of sentiments exists, especially upon theological subjects, and where morality is considered a part of religion and is, to some extent,

---

16. *The Common School Journal* (Boston), 1 August 1840, pp. 225-26.

modified by sectarian views, the difficulty and danger of attempting to introduce these subjects into our schools, according to one fixed and settled plan, to be devised by a central Board, must be obvious. The right to mould the political, moral, and religious opinions of his children is a right exclusively and jealously reserved by our laws to every parent; and for the government to attempt, directly or indirectly, as to these matters, to stand in the parent's place, is an undertaking of very questionable policy. Such an attempt cannot fail to excite a feeling of jealousy, with respect to our public schools, the results of which could not but be disastrous.[17]

One instance taken by the majority as a warning of the potential for tyranny by the board had to do with the adoption of an approved "school library" that all district schools were encouraged, though not required, to purchase. Such approved texts were the primary means by which the National Convention had attempted to shape education in France and that the Dutch educational reformers had used with significant impact early in the century. The Jeffersonian essayists had also made this a part of their program. It was perhaps inevitable that the school library developed under Mann's patronage would become one of the most controversial aspects of his program. Certainly it was so for the majority of the Committee on Education:

> It is professed, indeed, that the matter selected for this library will be free both from sectarian and political objections. Unquestionably, the Board will endeavour to render it so. Since, however, religion and politics, in this free country, are so intimately connected with every other subject, the accomplishment of that object is utterly impossible, nor would it be desirable, if possible. That must, indeed, be an uninteresting course of reading which would leave untouched either of these subjects; and he must be a heartless writer, who can treat religious or political subjects, without affording any indication of his political or religious opinions.

And then the majority states what has continued to be a major complaint about the treatment of religion in public school instruction. The context is Mann's repeated assertion that the school library was demonstrably neutral on religious matters because each title had been reviewed and approved by the entire Board, which included orthodox as well as Unitarian members.

> It is not sufficient, and it ought not to be, that a book contains

---

17. *The Common School Journal*, 1 August 1840, p. 230.

nothing which we believe to be false. If it omit to state what we believe to be true; if it founds itself upon vague generalities, which will equally serve the purpose of all reasoners, alike; this very omission to state what we believe to be the truth becomes, in our eyes, a fault of the most serious character. A book, upon politics, morals, or religion, containing no party or sectarian views, will be apt to contain no distinct views of any kind, and will be likely to leave the mind in a state of doubt and skepticism, much more to be deplored than any party or sectarian bias.[18]

As a Unitarian of his time, Mann considered himself a Christian who would preserve all that was pure, noble, and true of the teaching of Jesus Christ without the accretions of legend and speculative doctrine that, in his view, had been added by superstition and the calculation of a priestly caste. He was quite sincere in considering his views "nonsectarian." Teaching that sought to form a sincere piety directed toward the Creator, a morality based upon the example and ideals of Jesus Christ and conducive to civic peace and social righteousness—how could that "favor the tenets of particular sects"?

By and large his contemporaries agreed, including many who were themselves fully "orthodox." Those who did not agree insisted that what was presented was in fact a false religion, worse than no mention of religion at all, since it made no mention of sin as a corruption of human nature cutting us off from God and from our own happiness, nor of God's plan of salvation through Jesus Christ. By retaining only those aspects of Christianity with which Unitarians agreed, the proposed religious teaching was in fact identical with Unitarian teaching. Thus it *was* sectarian in the fullest sense. On the other hand, to teach about human sinfulness and God's redeeming grace could not be considered "sectarian," since these were simply facts accepted by virtually everyone and attested by the almost unchallenged authority of the Bible. Those who supported this position agreed that truly "sectarian" teaching should be excluded from the common school, but they sought to limit this characterization to such matters as baptism and church governance.

That this orthodox position did not prevail must be attributed largely to the theological confusion and "softness" of the orthodox party at that time, when so much of its energies were being devoted to evangelization of the cities, the West, and the world, with an inevitable popularization of doctrine in the interest of the broadest possible ac-

---

18. *The Common School Journal*, 1 August 1840, p. 228.

ceptance. The common school seemed part of the triumph of Christian benevolence, particularly when Mann urged that the Bible be read and morality taught in every school. Only the especially insightful, like Charles Hodge at Princeton, were able to foresee the rapid abandonment by public education of all connection with the essential beliefs of Christianity.

The majority summed up its opposition to the board and its initiatives in terms that had to do with a concept of society, with a commitment to a pluralism of goals of education and of the means of attaining these goals. From this perspective,

> the idea of the State controlling Education, whether by establishing a central Board, by allowing that Board to sanction a particular Library, or by organizing Normal Schools, seems to your Committee a great departure from the uniform spirit of our institutions,—a dangerous precedent, and an interference with a matter more properly belonging to those hands, to which our ancestors wisely intrusted it. It is greatly to be feared, that any attempt to form all our schools and all our teachers upon one model, would destroy all competition, all emulation, and even the spirit of improvement itself. When a large number of teachers and school committees are all aiming at improvement, as is doubtless the case, to a great extent, in this Commonwealth, improvements seem much more likely to be found out and carried into practice, than when the chief right of experimenting is vested in a central Board. With these views, your committee has come to the conclusion, that the interests of our Common Schools would rest upon a safer and more solid foundation if the Board of Education and the Normal Schools were abolished.[19]

The development of "normal schools" (teacher training institutions) in France, Germany, and the Netherlands was directly related to a new concept of the role of popular education. So long as elementary schools were simply to teach literacy skills, some basic arithmetic, and the catechism, Bible verses, or liturgical responses as religious instruction, they could be entrusted to anyone who was literate and of unexceptionable moral character. The church sexton, a disabled veteran, or even a literate tradesman might be the teacher; even better, it could be an aspirant to the ministry. Teaching was held to be a matter of passing on some skills one possessed as a result of one's own education

---

19. *The Common School Journal*, 1 August 1840, p. 229.

and of presiding over the memorization of some essential elements of the common religious heritage.

This was certainly a limited educational program, though it resulted in a high degree of literacy in New England and a respectable level in some parts of France, the German states, and the Netherlands. What it did not do, however, was to meet the new aspiration, growing out of Enlightenment views of society and of human nature, to use universal popular education as an instrument to achieve a number of social objectives that had nothing to do with literacy. These objectives included, as we have noted, a spirit of national unity, a commitment to the existing political order, and those "social and Christian virtues" that were considered necessary to ensure progress and the security of property.

If elementary schools—the very term *common school* expressed a political and social program—were to produce such profound transformations in the popular mentality, they must be taught by a new kind of teacher, one for whom the moral content of instruction was at least as significant as the basic skills. The first models for such teachers were the members of Roman Catholic teaching orders, the earliest of which were organized as instruments of the Counter-Reformation for the express purpose of educating and thereby converting Protestant children. These teaching brothers and sisters received a "formation" designed to enable them to rule their schools by moral authority rather than by the rod, and to have a profound impact upon the children entrusted to them. When teacher training institutions were established in the German states, it was with the significant title of "seminaries," and one of the first (and characteristically abortive) efforts of the French Revolution to create a "republican education" was the establishment of a national Ecole Normale Supèrieure in Paris.

Contemporary descriptions of normal schools during the nineteenth century, whether in Prussia, France, the Netherlands, or Massachusetts, almost never fail to stress the *moral* content of the formation of future teachers. A letter by Dr. Samuel Gridley Howe, one of Mann's chief allies and director of the Institution for the Blind in South Boston, was included as part of the minority report of the Committee of Education, supporting the board's initiatives. Howe wrote that he, like others, "entertained some theoretical objections to Normal Schools, as carried on by European governments," but that he was satisfied that the board's normal school at Lexington was unobjectionable in this regard, since "the moral nature is as much cultivated as the intellectual." The next year a report appeared in the *Common School Journal* from Cyrus

Peirce, principal of that institution, stressing that "there are no subjects in which scholars manifest more interest than in questions of morals." A biographical sketch of Peirce stressed "the especial attention he has paid to the *moral* culture of his pupils" and his opinion that "the common education of our schools has in it too little of the moral element."[20]

The stress on moral education in the normal school at Lexington had the same cause as the similar stress at Fontenay-aux-Roses in France under the Third Republic: it was a means of shaping young women into common school teachers whose convictions would be as clear and as winning as those of a teaching sister in a Catholic school.

James G. Carter, a predecessor of Mann as an education reformer in Massachusetts, had early identified the potential of teacher training as a means of having a profound impact upon popular education. In a series of articles published in 1824 and 1825 in the *Boston Patriot*, he urged a comprehensive scheme of education reform through state leadership. The key to the entire program was the training of teachers: "The character of the schools, and of course their political, moral and religious influence depend, almost solely, upon the character of the teachers." As a result,

> An institution for the education of teachers . . . would form a part, and a very important part, of the free-school system. It would be, moreover, precisely that portion of the system which should be under the direction of the State, whether the others are or not. . . . An institution for this purpose would become, by its influence on society, and particularly on the young, an engine to sway the public sentiment, the public morals, and the public religion, more powerful than any other in the possession of government. It should, therefore, be responsible immediately to them. . . . It should be emphatically the State's institution.[21]

And then he warned, "If it be not undertaken by the public and for public purposes, it will be undertaken by individuals for private purposes." But what invidious private purposes could Carter have been thinking of? After all, the "private" academies had been training teachers in a quite satisfactory manner, and Carter himself would attempt to operate

---

20. Henry Barnard, *American Educational Biography* (New York, 1859), pp. 428-29.
21. Carter, *Essays upon Popular Education, Containing a Particular Examination of the Schools of Massachusetts and an Outline of an Institution for the Instruction of Teachers* (Boston: Bowles & Dearborn, 1826), pp. 43, 49-50.

a private teacher training institution a few years later. Apparently such efforts were not what he had in mind.

It seems likely—though it cannot be proved—that his concern was with the potentially "sectarian" character of any teacher training not under state control. His own efforts would not be sectarian, to his own way of thinking, of course, but having once announced the tremendous power of teacher training to "sway the public sentiment, the public morals, and the public religion," he could not have failed to recognize that it was in the interest of the churches to exert their influence over the "engine" that promised to take over so much of their traditional role. It is common to find such oblique references in the writings of the education reformers to the ambitions and claims of organized religion, presumably because they recognized their own intention of moving the state into areas of public influence where religion had previously been almost unchallenged. As one commentator puts it succinctly, "the church was viewed with suspicion, but not the State."[22]

The normal school, then, played an important part in the efforts of Mann and other "liberal Christians" to promote a form of "common school religion" that was said to have no sectarian character but that was in fact consistent with their own beliefs and profoundly subversive of that of their Orthodox opponents. It was in the normal school, with its strong emphasis on the teaching of morality and on an atmosphere of liberal piety, that the teachers were formed upon whom the hopes of the education reformers rested. Training teachers was an effective way of avoiding the problems that a direct assault on local control of schools would have caused; it made it possible to argue, in all sincerity, that the common schools were under the direct oversight of local school committees elected by the parents and frequently chaired by an orthodox clergyman. The real content of public education would be determined by the emerging profession of teachers, shaped by state normal schools under control of the education reformers and not by the parents through their local representatives.

The effort to abolish the board of education in 1840 failed to pass the Massachusetts legislature; the principle of state leadership of education in the interest of a unitary "public" system was firmly established in Massachusetts. The sudden collapse of the not-unreasonable position reflected in the majority report of the Committee on Education can be explained only by the emergence of a new "threat" that encouraged re-

---

22. Rousas John Rushdoony, *The Messianic Character of American Education* (Nutley, N.J.: Craig Press, 1979), p. 39.

ligious liberals and orthodox, rural notables and urban financiers and intellectuals to make common cause in support of the common school as a program of the state rather than exclusively a concern of the town. The threat was immigration—specifically Irish Catholic immigration—and it quickly stilled the debate over the responsibility for popular education.

III. IMMIGRATION ENDS THE DEBATE

The inaugural address of Massachusetts governor Henry J. Gardner in 1855 (the year of the constitutional amendment with which we began) urged that

> The most prominent subject before our State and Nation at the present moment . . . concerns our foreign population;—the duties of republicanism towards them, its dangers from them . . . a foreign immigration in the ten years between 1840 and 1850 outnumbering the whole previous influx since the organization of the republic. . . . It is a great problem in statesmanship wisely to control the mingling of races into one nationality. The dominant race must regulate the incoming class. . . . Legislation must cooperate with time and circumstances in working out this decree of God, this axiom of political philosophy, this theory of nationality.

In the effort to create one nationality out of the mingled "races," Gardner told the legislators,

> Three of the most vital principles of a Republican Government are Spiritual Freedom, a Free Bible, and Free Schools. With these we cannot fail to have independent, upright and intelligent voters, and they necessarily insure a just, impartial and wise government. With their opposites, Spiritual Despotism, a Fettered Bible, or, more probably, no Bible at all, and Sectarian Schools, our liberties would exist but in name, and very soon but in history.

The first necessity for public policy, then, and the governor's first recommendation to the legislature, was "that amendment to the Constitution, which last year passed one stage of enactment, prohibiting the diversion of the educational funds of the State to the establishment or support of sectarian schools."[23]

In 1840, the primary policy issue in education was whether the

---

23. "Inaugural Address of His Excellency Henry J. Gardner," in *Acts and Resolves of 1855* (Boston, 1855), pp. 978-79.

state should seek to give direction to a system of popular education in the interest of some kind of uniformity of attitude, with many Protestants urging that the decision about the religious, moral, and political views to be taught in the schools must be determined by parents through their local elected school committees. But in the 1850s, the threat represented by Catholic immigrants to "Spiritual Freedom, a Free Bible, and Free Schools" forced a Protestant unity of support for a system of schools that had no room for such diversity.

Horace Bushnell, the deeply influential voice of liberal Congregationalism, wrote in 1853 that

> Evidently the time has now come, and the issue of life or death to common schools is joined for trial. The ground is taken, the flag is raised, and there is to be no cessation, till the question is forever decided, whether we are to have common schools in our country or not.... The common school is, in fact, an integral part of the civil order.... An application against common schools is so far an application for the dismemberment and reorganization of the civil order of the state.... Common schools are nurseries thus of a free republic, private schools of factions, cabals, agrarian laws and contests of force....[24]

The Catholic immigrants under the influence of their clergy, Bushnell argued, were guilty of gross ingratitude in refusing to accept the common school.

> We bid them welcome as they come, and open to their free possession all the rights of our American citizenship. They, in turn, forbid their children to be Americans, pen them as foreigners to keep them so, and train them up in the speech of Ashdod among us. And then, to complete the affront, they come to our legislatures demanding it, as their right, to share in funds collected by a taxing of the whole people, and to have these funds applied to the purpose of keeping their children from being Americans. Our only answer to such demands is, "No! take your place with us in our common schools, and consent to be Americans, or else go back to Turkey, where Mohammedans, Greeks, Armenians, Jews are walled up by the laws themselves.... I said go back to Turkey—that is unnecessary. If we do not soon prepare a state of Turkish order and felicity here, by separating and folding our children thus, in the stringent limits of religious non-

---

24. Bushnell, "Common Schools" (1853), in *American Writings on Popular Education: The Nineteenth Century*, ed. Rush Welter (Indianapolis: Bobbs-Merrill, 1971), p. 177.

acquaintance and consequent animosity, it will be because the laws of human nature and society have failed.[25]

The only preventative to this deplorable possibility, according to Bushnell, was common schools teaching a common religion and morality, "such a plan as will be Christian, and will not infringe, in the least, upon the tenets of either party, the Protestant or the Catholic. It has been done in Holland." He was, of course, unaware that this attempt, in the Netherlands, would lead to a political struggle of seven decades and an eventual "pacification" providing for separate Catholic, Protestant, and public schools.

In Bushnell's formulation, what had been the bitter struggle between liberal and orthodox Protestants is brushed aside and they are subsumed into a single "party," standing over against the Catholic newcomers with their unreasonable demands to preserve their distinctive understanding of the religious basis of morality. To this end, someone should "prepare a book of Christian morality, distinct from a doctrine of religion or a faith, which shall be taught indiscriminately to all the scholars."[26]

The error made by Bushnell and many others in the Protestant elite, one may say, was a failure of sociological imagination, a failure to recognize how determined the immigrants were not only to preserve certain aspects of their native culture but also to see their children become "Americans"—and to appreciate the assimilative power of the society itself. As has occurred so often in modern times, the power of schools to *educate* was overestimated, to the confusion of their function of imparting *instruction*.

Over the next decades, and starting with the urban centers that experienced the impact of immigration most directly, the mission of public education to create citizens on a uniform pattern was developed and elaborated. Historian David B. Tyack has described this search for "the one best system" of popular schooling. In his judgment, "The search for the one best system has ill-served the pluralistic character of American society."[27]

Most school leaders of the nineteenth century asserted that class-consciousness was wrong and that the common school should combat group divisiveness of all kinds—class, ethnic, religious, or

---

25. Bushnell, "Common Schools," p. 185.
26. Bushnell, "Common Schools," p. 191.
27. Tyack, *The One Best System: A History of American Urban Education* (Cambridge: Harvard University Press, 1974), p. 11.

political. This concern with group conflict, with threats to the existing order, pervaded their rhetoric on the purposes of public education.[28]

In particular, control or influence by parents who stood outside of the American mainstream was to be deplored. As one New York reformer wrote in 1896, it was inadvisable

> in a city like this so impregnated with foreign influence, languages and ideas that the school should be controlled locally; for in many localities, the influences that would control would be unquestionably un-American. In some districts there are vast throngs of foreigners where one scarcely hears a word of English spoken, where the mode of living is repugnant to every American.[29]

This fear that the "American experiment" would somehow fly apart if not held together by a common form of schooling teaching common values and loyalties, this distrust of the assimilating power of American society, has remained a powerful undercurrent in discussions of educational policy, even though its premises have been disproved resoundingly by our national experience, not least by the actual results of parochial and other "sectarian" education.

IV. THE ISSUES LEFT UNRESOLVED

The debate over popular education was prematurely hushed as the new immigration made the disagreements of Unitarians, Arminians, and Calvinists fade into seeming unimportance. Protestants closed ranks to insist that the newcomers conform to a single American pattern, though before the immigrants came, the lack of such a pattern had seemed a major problem. The common school—until then the cause of a few enthusiasts—became the cornerstone of a policy of forced assimilation.

Other modernizing nations pursued different options for popular education. In Prussia, strong and systematic state leadership took great care to accommodate religious traditions, with almost all elementary schools designated as either Protestant or Catholic, and local clergy playing a major role in the oversight responsibilities. Many "public" schools were staffed and run by religious teaching orders until the struggles over the *ècole laique* of the last quarter of the nineteenth century,

---

28. Tyack, *The One Best System*, p. 73.
29. Tyack, *The One Best System*, p. 151.

which constituted a true conflict of faiths, with a militant secularism (nurtured by Romantic and Positivist political thinking) seeking to use the schools to create an alternative to religious belief. In Britain the lead was taken by voluntary associations, mostly either Church of England or Dissenting or Roman Catholic, which then received financial support from local and central government. In the Netherlands—the example cited by Bushnell and many others who favored a deeply religious but nonsectarian instruction—the effort to define the appropriate content and control of popular education was, even more than in France or Britain, the preeminent issue around which political debate came to revolve.

Popular education made an early start in the Netherlands, with a functioning system in advance of any other nation by the end of the Napoleonic wars. The Dutch education reformers shared in the nation-building aspirations we have already noted, but they mediated them through the strong Dutch tradition of liberal Protestantism. Elementary schools were expected to teach a "Christianity above differences of belief," with an emphasis on God as Creator and on morality, remarkably similar to the program recommended by Horace Mann.

By mid-century, however, the consensus that supported this approach—so much admired by foreign visitors—had fallen apart. Ironically, the new Constitution forced through by the Liberals in 1848 was the downfall of their educational program, since it brought new social classes, in which traditional Calvinism and Roman Catholicism were predominant, into political life. The schools were the issue around which these new classes became mobilized politically, in a process Jim Skillen has described in a thoughtful article. Orthodox Calvinists, increasingly militant in the wake of several secessions from the semiestablished Hervormde Kerk, organized their own schools, as did Catholics, and both groups joined forces to agitate for financial support for their schools. Freedom to organize nonpublic schools, a right won in the 1850s, was limited, they said, without equal access to funding. By the 1880s the growing electorate gave these groups enough power to form governments and begin to provide tax support to nonpublic schools. Since the *pacificatie* of 1917, confessional schools have enjoyed equal support in every way. Some seventy percent of Dutch elementary enrollment is in what we would call nonpublic schools. Every school is expected to offer some form of "worldview" instruction, whether traditionally religious or humanistic, even under the new educational legislation that has just gone into effect.

In the Netherlands, then, as in France and Britain (and, to a lesser extent, in Germany) the question of control and "religious" content of popular education was a source of controversy for a hundred years or more. This debate did not take place with anything like the same degree of intensity in the United States, largely, as I have suggested, because the immigration that gathered force in the 1840s, just as the education reformers were advocating a program of "neutral" education to serve the agenda of the state, gave them an easy and indeed unanticipated victory. A second factor, which I have discussed elsewhere, involves the nature of evangelical Protestantism in the nineteenth century.

Was this nation fortunate to be spared that debate? Not necessarily. Indeed, it might be argued that we are experiencing a *lutte scolaire*, a *schoolstrijd* today. Without attempting to weigh the might-have-beens of American history, it is worth noting some of the issues we have not debated or resolved, issues that were in fact alluded to in the report of the Education Committee in 1840 and that continue to plague us today.

1. What role should explicit and implicit teaching of values and loyalties—what we have called *education* as contrasted with *instruction*—have in the program of elementary schools? Is there such a thing as a value-free school, and, if there is, is that to be desired?

There is tremendous confusion on this question. For example, critics of our public schools often say that they fail to teach character and values, then turn around and say—in the context of criticizing "Values Clarification"—that schools should leave the teaching of values to the family and the church. Defenders switch with equal inconsequence from extolling the character-forming supremacy of public schools to hiding behind the First Amendment when asked to discuss what kind of character they seek to form.

In fairness to Horace Mann, he was very clear about the importance of the cultivation of virtue in schools; unlike more recent social reformers, he did not believe that it was enough to manipulate social conditions through rewards and "counterincentives" so that the exercise of virtue would be unnecessary. He and his allies (and their counterparts in France and the Netherlands) believed that it was sufficient to stress moral exhortation deriving, ultimately, from the Stoic lists of virtues and vices and to inculcate national loyalty with little sense of the role of traditions and social groups, much less of religious beliefs and institutions, in the formation of the desired character.

It is curious that there is considerable demand in conservative circles today for a return to what was the essentially statist program of

Mann and the other reformers, with no apparent advance in understanding of how values and loyalties are formed.

2. At what level should decisions be made about the content of schooling? Should these be matters for national or state policy, for the local community, or for the family? Horace Mann's contemporaries assumed that the local community would continue to play the major role, as it had since colonial times, though the majority of the Education Committee was, as we have seen, prescient in detecting the seeds of a larger state role in the measures promoted by Mann.

One of the consequences of modernization with the impetus that it gives to diversity of beliefs, values, goals, "lifestyles," and assumptions about raising children is that schools that attempt to reflect their local communities, the residential areas in which presumably all children are to attend the same school, are educationally incoherent and incapable of providing the sort of moral order conducive to the development of character or even the maintenance of discipline.

As an alternative to this incoherence, some would have the state define more aggressively the goals and content of schooling. This is at least a possible implication of the stress Secretary of Education William Bennett has placed on an essential content to which all students should be exposed.

In some respects, ironically, this has already been occurring, though in a manner and with an intent to which he might well object. In the mid-seventies, for example, my office did a great deal to change the way in which sex roles are presented in the public schools of Massachusetts. We formed advisory committees in each part of the Commonwealth, made up primarily of individuals who advocated changing the expectations of girls (and boys) concerning their future occupations and roles in society. Under their auspices we provided training to thousands of teachers; distributed thousands of guides, posters, brochures, and other materials; and monitored the efforts of school systems to "eliminate sex stereotypes" and to "promote gender-fair education." In addition to providing special "career education" classes, we called for the infusion of these themes into all aspects of the curriculum. Our technical assistance and training activities were backed up with vigorous monitoring and enforcement and supported with state funding; we granted two million dollars to Boston alone to develop and infuse such programs. We had no difficulty dismissing the few voices raised in protest as examples of the endemic "sexism" of our society. Whether in fact our efforts were more than a sideshow to the massive shifts taking place in the society at that time it would be difficult to say, but the intention to redefine the goals of schooling through the exercise of state leadership was certainly there.

The present "school reform movement" seems to rely heavily upon an increased assertion by the several states of leadership in and authority over the content of schooling. On the other hand, the growing "home schooling" movement is an attempt to assert the opposite extreme of decision-making about the schooling of children, the unmediated intervention of their parents. While there is a superficial attractiveness to the idea of keeping children under a direct and exclusive parental influence for as long as possible, I believe that it ignores the reality of the social nature of our existence and, from a Christian perspective, is based upon a theological error as well. But that is another discussion.

The ideal, it seems to me, is for the decisions about schooling to be made by communities that are diverse enough to reflect the economic and racial/ethnic diversity of our society but similar enough with respect to the goals of education to create schools that are educationally and morally coherent, schools where character and abiding loyalties can be formed. Sociologist James Coleman wrote recently in the *Phi Delta Kappan* about the "intergenerational closure" characteristic of such schools, using as examples one school in a small Appalachian town and another school serving mostly the University of Chicago. In both cases the parents constitute a community that parallels and supports the community of the school.

3. To what extent is there an overriding state interest in the uniformity of the values and loyalties taught to young children in elementary schools? Is this, as nineteenth-century Liberals in France and the Netherlands contended, a matter of supreme significance for national unity and progress? Put in the blunt terms that were heard occasionally, does the child belong to the state or to the family?

John Stuart Mill argued in *On Liberty* that

> A general State education is a mere contrivance for molding people to be exactly alike one another: and as the mold in which it casts them is that which pleases the predominant power in the government... in proportion as it is efficient and successful, it establishes a despotism over the mind, leading by natural tendency to one over the body.

Mill makes the common mistake of giving too much credit to the power of formal schooling to shape students for whom the family and the broader society are far more effective agents of socialization, but it should be noted that he expresses what was in fact the *aspiration* of Mann and other education reformers in the Liberal tradition.

It could be argued that this issue has been resolved in the United States by the 1925 ruling of the Supreme Court in *Pierce v. Society of Sisters*, which overturned an Oregon law that required children to be sent to *public* schools. The Court held that

> The fundamental theory of liberty upon which all governments in this Union repose excludes any general power of the State to standardize its children by forcing them to accept instruction from public teachers only. The child is not the mere creature of the State; those who nurture him and direct his destiny have the right, coupled with the high duty, to recognize and prepare him for additional obligations.

Although there is not a true "public school monopoly" in the United States—that is, a monopoly of the right to provide formal education to children of the sort which was attempted (but soon abandoned) under the Third Republic in France and that exists in the Soviet Union and many other nations—it is to be regretted that this possibility has been excluded in the United States through a legal ruling rather than through a political process. The resolution of issues of high public interest through a political process is, after all, the real school of citizenship, and it is arguable that the political passivity of many Americans is the result of the removal of issues of such basic import for every parent from the sphere of political debate.

4. If the state does not have a right to the monopoly of educating young children, what range of diversity can we tolerate in teaching about values and loyalties? What are the outer limits of this diversity, beyond which society is unwilling to accept idiosyncratic teaching?

The charge brought by Horace Bushnell against the schools organized by Roman Catholic clergy for the children of the faithful was that they detracted from the loyalty those children should owe to their American nationality. The familiar specter of the Pope as a "foreign potentate" was raised by Bushnell and others as a primary argument for the common school. In the same vein, the state of Oregon, in defending its law requiring attendance at public schools, suggested that the effect of private schools would be to promote the claims of "the religion to which they belonged" as "superior to the claims of the United States."

The discussion about educational pluralism continues to be bedeviled by contemporary versions of this chestnut. Would you allow a

Nazi school? Would you allow a white racist school? Would you allow a Black Muslim school? Would you allow a school that taught the biological inferiority of women? Would you allow a school that taught that women can find their greatest fulfillment in motherhood? Would you allow a school that taught that homosexual practices are unnatural? And so forth, coming ever closer to the description of some nonpublic schools already in existence.

This is not the place to attempt to answer these questions but simply to suggest that it is good for a society to be confronting such questions, healthy in its implications for the state of political discourse.

The debate over the purposes and the control of popular education was hushed by the need of the Protestant majority to unite in support of a concept of the common school as a powerful instrument of assimilation of millions of immigrants, or of their children. The debate was hushed, but the issues were not resolved. They have reemerged in our own time in a confused way—confused because we have so little tradition of political discourse about the goals of education.

During the nineteenth and early twentieth centuries, religious minorities were free to organize their own schools, at their own expense, provided they did not press for public financial support. Thousands of such schools were founded and supported with sacrificial efforts. By 1920 there were nearly six thousand Catholic parochial schools educating 1,700,000 students, together with over a thousand Lutheran schools, some six hundred Seventh-day Adventist schools, and hundreds of other "sectarian" schools.

In a sense, then, the demand for religiously distinctive schooling was tolerated but at the same time marginalized. Meanwhile government-controlled schooling enjoyed not only a monopoly on tax support but also the prestige of its role as the designated shrine of Americanism. It became, as Rockne McCarthy and others have noted, the equivalent of an established church, and it has suffered the fate of the Church of England and similar establishments in recent years: it has become the target of innumerable critics while suffering almost as much from the ho-hum attitude of its own officials. It is mocked as irrelevant and ineffective and accused of wielding unlimited sinister power. Increasing evidence suggests that American public schools are in fact experiencing a crisis remarkably akin to secularization, in which the faith claims upon which they rest cease to carry conviction.

V. RENEWING THE DEBATE IN MASSACHUSETTS

It was in Massachusetts and New York that the debate over the purpose and control of education was most dramatically cut off by the shock of immigration, and it is the same states that currently have the largest state-funded programs to provide a measure of diversity within public education. I refer to the "magnet school" programs that are supported at a level of approximately $15 million in each state.

In Massachusetts we are groping back toward a renewal of the debate that was cut off so abruptly a century and a half ago. We are conducting a series of practical experiments with educational diversity that to some extent grapple with the four unresolved issues outlined above.

Briefly, magnet schools are a means of complying with race desegregation requirements through encouraging students to attend integrated schools on a voluntary basis. Characteristically such schools offer enriched resources and a specialized program, and often make a somewhat elitist appeal designed to encourage white parents to keep their children in urban public schools.

The seventy or so magnet schools in Massachusetts are rather different. In the first place, we have been emphatic that these schools may not adopt selective admission policies, though they may offer programs of supplemental challenge to academically talented students as part of an effort to meet each child's educational needs. At the elementary level we discourage the attempt to provide resources that are superior to those in other schools, focusing instead on encouraging the greatest possible development of the *distinctiveness* of each school. Since the program of studies at the elementary level is relatively fixed, this has meant an emphasis upon the distinctive philosophy or educational mission of each school, which in turn has required a process of working through the expectations of parents and staff to a common understanding of their goals.

In short, we see the magnet school and in general the promotion of choice in public education as a way of creating educationally and— yes—morally coherent schools. As racially diverse parents and staff work together to define what they mean by a "traditional school" or a "child-centered school" or a "developmental school" or however they define the common vision that draws them to a commitment to this particular option among others, they become the sort of community that should support and give direction to education. They achieve the "intergenerational closure" described by Coleman.

As to the second "unresolved question," concerning the level at which decisions about schooling should be made, we would suggest that such decisions should be worked out through intensive interaction in the "local community," making note of the fact, however, that this community is no longer the New England village but rather the voluntary community formed by those committed to a particular school. The role of the state is to help to create the framework within which this process can take place and to guard against injustice. Ensuring racial integration is one way of assuring that poor children do not end up disproportionately concentrated in less-favored or less-effective schools. The role of parents—and it is a more effective form of "empowerment" than the farcical parent councils to which we have devoted so much effort—is to choose the school in which they will place their children and to which they will commit whatever talents and energies they have available.

Having arrived (as an unanticipated consequence of another objective, desegregation) at a conviction of the power of choice and of the "local community" formed by choices, it has become possible for us to begin to answer the first question. In the context of choice it is feasible to say that of course values and loyalties are taught in schools, implicitly if not explicitly, and so they should be taught as openly and unapologetically as possible. It has been a lack of choice that has given us so many difficulties with the training of character!

The educationally and morally incoherent schools so common today have been produced by a public education system that calls on each school to find a lowest common denominator of commitments and convictions to avoid giving offense to *any* parent. What a futile and finally unnecessary restriction! In the context of choice, of freely made commitments to a particular school on the part of parents and staff alike, it is possible to develop the distinctiveness that alone can support the development of virtue.

So far have we come. The third question, concerning the interest of the state in assuring uniformity in the teaching of values and loyalties is, as already noted, not presented in its pure form in American education. Our commitment in Massachusetts to promoting diversity and choice is based upon a conviction that it is unnecessary to promote a single public school model over against the diversity of nonpublic schools. It is based also upon the experience that even the educational goals we are most determined to promote, such as respect for people of other races, can be achieved in a wide variety of ways and are most likely to be achieved in schools that elicit commitment and energy from staff, parents, and students. Thus whether a school is "child-centered" or "traditional," for example, has less to do with the racial attitudes developed within it than whether it has been freely chosen and is engaged in an on-going process of developing its distinctiveness.

An answer to the fourth question, about the outer limits of the diversity we can permit (at least in tax-supported schools), will have to emerge from the process of differentiation and on-going magnet school development in which we are now engaged. It seems to me that we have not even approached those limits thus far. The main difficulty is persuading school people that they can be bolder, that uniformity is no longer necessary, that they can talk freely about values and character and their educational goals.

We have a very long way to go, even in the dozen Massachusetts cities with which I am working, before we will be able to say that public education is truly responsive to the pluralism of American society. At most our experiences show that parents and students want choice, that they are capable of sophisticated choices (though often on the basis of school characteristics that seem of little importance to education experts and researchers, such as the personal integrity of the principal or the warmth of the "school climate"), and that *having chosen* increases commitment to a school, *being chosen* improves morale in a school, and *not being chosen* is the most effective incentive for improved teacher and administrator performance that we have yet discovered!

Surely *this* is how citizens are to be educated in a democracy—through learning to make choices that lead to commitments, through sharing in the "local communities" that can form around a freely chosen school, through learning and teaching in schools that are coherent expressions of such communities. This vision, imperfectly realized as it is so far, is at once higher and more realistic than that of Horace Mann and the other education reformers, of forming citizens on a single mold through schools whose objectives are set by an elite in conscious despite of the convictions and loyalties of families and the religious and social institutions through which their participation in the nation is mediated.

Public Schools and Public Justice: The Past, the Present, and the Future

Rockne M. McCarthy

The United States is in the midst of a major movement to reform education. The renewal is motivated in part by a series of reports that have critically evaluated the condition of public education at every level.[1] But will today's soul-searching encompass a reevaluation of the commonly held assumptions regarding the meaning and structure of public education in a pluralist, democratic society such as America? It is my conviction that such a reevaluation is long overdue.

In this paper, I would like to look first at the ways in which public elementary and secondary education in the United States came to be institutionalized in government-owned, -operated, and -funded secular

---

1. Among the many reports are the following: National Commission on Excellence in Education, *A Nation at Risk: The Imperative for Education Reform* (Washington: U.S. Government Printing Office, 1983); Task Force on Education for Economic Growth, *Action for Excellence* (Denver: Education Commission of the States, 1983); Task Force on Federal Elementary and Secondary Education Policy, *Making the Grade* (New York: Twentieth Century Fund, 1983); National Science Board Commission on Precollege Education in Mathematics, Science and Technology, *Educating Americans for the 21st Century* (Washington: National Science Foundation, 1984); National Endowment for the Humanities, *To Reclaim a Legacy: A Report on the Humanities in Higher Education* (Washington: U.S. Government Printing Office, 1984); National Institute of Education, *Involvement in Learning: Realizing the Potential of American Higher Education* (Washington: U.S. Government Printing Office, 1984); and Project on Redefining the Meaning and Purpose of Baccalaureate Degrees, *Integrity in the College Curriculum* (Washington: Association of American Colleges, 1985).

schools. I will argue that this development reflects an essentially nonpluralist understanding of public education. It results in a monopolist educational establishment that discriminates against the diversity of schools within the public community.

Although a monopolist structure for public education did not emerge in the United States until the nineteenth century, it has become a reigning paradigm, the validity of which is assumed by many to be self-evident. The historical record demonstrates, however, that the nonpluralist structure is the product of political and ideological choices that were less self-evident than they were self-serving for majoritarian interests.

In the second part of this paper, I would like to move on to analyze the "crisis of legitimacy" that the public school establishment is undergoing today. I understand this crisis to stem in part from the awareness that we live in a post- Enlightenment age in which people increasingly challenge the possibility of secular (nonreligious/value-free) education and in part from the inherent tension between a monopolist educational establishment and the diversity of educational views that exists in modern society.

In the last section of this essay I would like to focus on the need to move toward genuine educational pluralism and the disestablishment of the present public school monopoly. I will not be suggesting that the government has no legitimate role to play in education. In this context I will be using the term *disestablishment* to refer to a change in the present monopolist *structure* of public education. I believe a pluralist structural reform is necessary to produce education that is truly "public" and that meets the democratic norms for a just political community.

In the United States the present nonpluralist educational establishment (elementary and secondary education in particular) stands in contrast to an honorable history of pluralist disestablishment of churches. Some European states still support monopolist ecclesiastical establishments, tolerating other churches but providing them no funds. The United States has no such established church, of course, but its monopolist public school establishment functions in a similar manner, tolerating other schools only if they receive most of their funding from private sources.

Genuine educational freedom demands that we disestablish the present monopolist structure and replace it with a pluralist system. This will result in a more comprehensive definition of public education—a definition that encompasses a fuller range of schools worthy of public support. But before such democratic reform can take place it will be necessary to define (1) a more pluralist view of the state, (2) the nature of public responsibility for education, (3) parental responsibility for and freedom of choice in education, (4) the rights, privileges, and responsibilities of founding organizations and cooperating institutions in the educational enterprise, and (5) ways to improve excellence in education. I will address each of these points briefly.

THE NINETEENTH CENTURY: THE ESTABLISHMENT

In our society it is not too difficult to identify the characteristic features of a public school. Public ownership, public control, public financial support, and secular education are some of the traits that come to mind. In the prior history of American education, however, the meaning of *public* education has been far more ambiguous than it is today—something historians have only recently come to realize.[2]

As Bernard Bailyn's insightful historiographical study of American educational history reveals, there has been a tendency to read modern definitions back into the past. He points out that our treatment of *public* is perhaps the best example of this anachronistic tendency. Indeed, one of the main weaknesses of the history written by Ellwood Cubberley and other "educational missionaries" at the turn of the century was their assumption that the seeds of modern public education were to be found in the seventeenth century. They came to this conclusion because "it was the 'public' aspect of education that most involved their energies and that framed their vision: 'public' vs. 'private,' the state as equalizer and guarantor, assuring through tax-supported, free, publically maintained and publically controlled schools the level of education that made democracy effective."[3]

A more objective reading of history reveals, Bailyn argues, that the "modern conception of public education, the very idea of a clean

---

2. For much of the historical material in this section I have relied on my previous writing in the following two books: Rockne McCarthy, Donald Oppewal, Walfred Peterson, and Gordon Spykman, *Society, State and Schools: A Case for Structural and Confessional Pluralism* (Grand Rapids: Eerdmans, 1981); and Rockne McCarthy, James Skillen, and William Harper, *Disestablishment a Second Time: Genuine Pluralism for American Schools* (Grand Rapids: Eerdmans, 1982).

3. Bailyn, *Education in the Forming of American Society: Needs and Opportunities of Study* (Chapel Hill, N.C.: University of North Carolina Press, 1960), p. 10. Lawrence Cremin also discusses turn-of-the-century educational historiography in *The Wonderful World of Ellwood Patterson Cubberly* (New York: Teachers College Press, 1965).

line of separation between 'private' and 'public,' was unknown before the end of the eighteenth century." He further demonstrates that the emergence of the modern conception of public education is directly related to nineteenth-century "changes in the role of the state as well as in the general institutional character of society."[4] This is an extremely important observation, because it alerts us to the structural issue of the relationship between the state and schools. It also raises the question of the respective rights of these two institutions as well as the rights of parents and students in a pluralist, democratic society, issues to which I will return in the last part of this essay.

Bailyn contends that the origins of the clean line of separation between "public" and "private" education can be traced back to a complex nest of issues in the nation's early modern history. While this is true, we need not dig too deeply into that history to discover that although the terms *public* and *private* were used to describe schools in the colonial and early national periods, they referred only to the ownership and management of schools and not at all to two features that today characterize public education: public funding and a secular perspective.

In the nineteenth century, both government and nongovernment schools typically charged tuition and received public funds to pursue their educational objectives. It was common for nongovernment schools to receive public funds in the form of local taxes, allocations from state school funds, and land grants. Independent pay schools, academies, and church schools were called public schools because they were understood to serve the public interest by preparing children for responsible public life, and the community stood to benefit if students attended the school of their choice.[5]

During this same period in Boston, New York, Philadelphia, and elsewhere, both government and nongovernment schools taught from a religious perspective. Government-controlled schools reflected a Protestant consensus, and other publicly funded nongovernment schools were organized by specific churches or religious groups. While the distinction between public and private schools was considered relevant in matters of ownership and management, it was considered irrelevant in such matters as religious education and funding. In the early nineteenth century, few sharp lines between "public" and "pri-

---

4. Bailyn, *Education in the Forming of American Society*, p. 11.
5. See *Turning Points in American Educational History*, ed. David B. Tyack (Lexington, Mass.: Xerox College Publishing, 1967), p. 120; Carl F. Kaestle, *Pillars of the Republic: Common Schools and American Society, 1780-1860* (New York: Hill & Wang, 1983), pp. 51-52.

vate" education existed because "public" implied performance of broad social functions.

In the early national period, the significant changes occurring in rural schooling were somewhat different from those occurring in urban schooling. According to Carl F. Kaestle, the dynamic aspect of rural education during this period was expanding enrollment, whereas urban education was more affected by a shift from diverse independent pay and charity schools to consolidated free schools. As academies and other independent pay schools declined in numbers and became increasingly elite and expensive, charity schools expanded and became the vehicles for pedagogical, organizational, and financial reforms. By the 1820s in several urban areas a single school organization "became dominant, controlling the bulk of charity schools and attaining favored status for financial assistance from the city and state."[6] In urban areas public education was coming to mean nonsectarian (eventually secular) education, with schools financed and run by a common school system.

The example par excellence of this development is the school system in New York City. Here the emergence of a clean line of separation between public and private schools clearly reflected political and ideological choices. The gradual separation came in the midst of two controversies involving the New York Free School Society and its successor, the New York Public School Society.

The first conflict involved the Free School Society and a school operated by a Baptist church. At the turn of the nineteenth century, a diverse collection of schools in New York City was funded by allocations from the state's "permanent school fund," which had been established in 1805 to support public education. Money was allocated from the fund to a variety of the city's schools (church schools, charity schools, etc.) on the basis of the number of students given free education by each.

We need not go into the details of the conflict between the Society and the Baptist school because it is documented well elsewhere.[7] For our purposes here it is enough to note that the conflict resulted in a

---

6. Kaestle, *Pillars of the Republic*, p. 57.
7. See in particular John Webb Pratt, *Religion, Politics and Diversity: The Church-State Theme in New York History* (Ithaca, N.Y.: Cornell University Press, 1967); Vincent P. Lannie, *Public Money and Parochial Education: Bishop Hughes, Governor Seward, and the New York School Controversy* (Cleveland: Case Western Reserve University Press, 1968); and Diane Ravitch, *The Great School Wars: New York City, 1805-1973* (New York: Basic Books, 1974).

change in the educational funding procedure from a policy based on proportionality to a monopolist policy. For the first time in New York City only the schools of the Free School Society received public funds; all other schools were denied public support.

A consensus so dominated the city in the 1820s that citizens were willing to publicly support just one school system and give it the task of educating children into the "common faith" of the people. The controversy did not, however, result in a clean line of separation between public and private schools. Despite the fact that the Society changed its name to the Public School Society, it remained a private philanthropic organization run by a self-perpetuating board of trustees.

The New York Public School Society was again involved in a controversy over public funding in the 1840s. In this conflict it became clear that the "common faith" of the people was really the "common faith" of the Protestant majority in New York City. In the end it was the self-serving political and ideological choices of majoritarian interests that defined the modern meaning and structure of public education.

By 1840 large-scale immigration of Irish Catholics to New York City produced a significant ethnic community with its own newspapers, social clubs, and professional elite. Catholics refused to send their children to the Society's schools because they clearly reflected a Protestant world-and-life view. The Catholics perceived the very reading of Scripture from the King James Bible without note or comment as fostering the Protestant doctrine of private interpretation of Scripture. In addition, they objected to the use of sectarian prayers and hymns, the presence of objectionable schoolbooks, and a deistic educational perspective. Catholics refused to attend the city's public schools because they could not do so with a clear conscience. In the end the basic issue, as they saw it, was the violation of the rights of conscience and citizenship.

In 1840 the governor of New York, William Henry Seward, responded to the complaints of growing numbers of Catholic citizens by recommending "the establishment of schools in which they [immigrant children] may be instructed by teachers speaking the same language with themselves and professing the same faith."[8] Seward was concerned for both the immigrants' rights and the large number of their children who were not being educated. He felt he had to address this situation because "no system of education could answer the ends of a republic

---

8. Seward, quoted by Glyndon G. Van Deusen in "Seward and the School Question Reconsidered," *Journal of American History* 52 (1965): 313.

but one which secures education for all."⁹

The Catholics in New York City were encouraged by the governor's proposal. Led by the newly appointed Bishop John Hughes, they responded by pressing the claim to a proportional share of the common school fund to support their schools.¹⁰

In a written petition to the Common Council of New York City, Bishop Hughes argued that a monopoly of state funds for education was controlled by a private corporation which had as one of its goals the "early religious instruction" of children.¹¹ In his oral presentation before the Council, Hughes pointed out the bias against Catholics in this religious training. The Bishop stressed that Catholics resented having to support schools that violated the religious conscience of their children. He did not object to all groups sharing in the common school fund; he objected only to the educational monopoly of the Public School Society. Hughes ended his oral comments by appealing to the Council not to

> take from Catholics their portion of the fund by taxation, and hand it over to those who do not give them an equivalent in return. Let those who can receive the advantages of these schools; but as Catholics cannot, do not tie them to a system which is intended for the advantage of a class of society of which they form one-third, but from which system they can receive no benefit.¹²

The Public School Society was represented before the Common Council by two prominent New York attorneys. One of them, Hiram Ketchum, was a long-time trustee of the Society. Ketchum rejected Hughes's charge that the Society's schools engaged in offensive sectarian education. Sectarian teaching, he argued, was completely inappropriate in a common school supported by public funds. At the same time, he stressed that public education must inculcate universal

---

9. Seward, quoted by Lannie in *Public Money and Parochial Education*, p. 22.

10. By 1839 the Roman Catholic Church had established seven Catholic schools in the city with more than 5,000 students enrolled. The schools were open to all students.

11. Bishop Hughes's evidence came from the Public School Society's 1827 Report. See Hughes, "The Petition of the Catholics of the City of New York" (September 21, 1840), reprinted in *American Writings on Popular Education: The Nineteenth Century*, ed. Rush Welter (Indianapolis: Bobbs-Merrill, 1971), p. 104.

12. Hughes, quoted by Lannie in *Public Money and Parochial Education*, p. 78.

principles of virtue and morality. This was the legitimate responsibility and task of a common school such as the Public School Society:

> We have the right to declare moral truths, and this community gives us that right—not the law, but as my friend says, public sentiment.... We thus undertake in these public schools to furnish this secular education, embracing as it does, not solely and exclusively the common rudiments of learning, but also a knowledge of good morals, and those common sanctions of religion which are acknowledged by every body.[13]

In the debate before the Common Council, Hughes and Ketchum were speaking past each other. Each rested his argument on a completely different understanding of the nature of religion. Hughes defined religion holistically. From his perspective, sectarian doctrine was an essential part of every religious perspective. Any effort to appeal to so-called universal or neutral moral precepts was just another form of sectarianism—in the case of the Public School Society, the sectarianism of infidelity (deistic rationalism). Ketchum, on the other hand, understood religion dualistically. He believed there was an essential difference between a collection of general moral principles and the specific doctrinal beliefs of the denominations. He believed it was possible to teach universal principles of virtue and morality in a nonsectarian way.

Ketchum's argument essentially mirrors those of Thomas Jefferson and Horace Mann.[14] And like Jefferson and Mann, Ketchum

---

13. Ketchum, quoted by Lannie in *Public Money and Parochial Education*, p. 83.

14. Jefferson's plan to establish a system of public elementary and secondary schools is outlined in a bill ("Bill for the More General Diffusion of Knowledge") he presented to the Virginia legislature in 1779. For a full examination and critique of Jefferson's educational perspective, see *Disestablishment a Second Time*, pp. 15-29. See also David Little, "The Origins of Perplexity: Civil Religion and Moral Belief in the Thought of Thomas Jefferson," in *American Civil Religion*, ed. Russell E. Richey and Donald G. Jones (New York: Harper & Row, 1974), pp. 199-200. Jefferson's vision for a nonsectarian system of public education was based largely on the assumption that sectarian opinions and doctrines could not "pass the sure, simple standard of common sense." It is precisely for that reason, argues David Little, that Jefferson believed sectarian opinion and doctrines "should be set apart and fenced off from the world of action, the world of civil responsibility, by a 'wall of separation.' It was *not*, as we are so often told, that Jefferson honored and respected differences of opinion so much that he erected his famous wall. On the contrary, it was because he honored and respected them so little" ("Thomas

was completely unaware that his views were simply another sectarian opinion or doctrine. They all assumed their beliefs were authenticated by common sense and therefore had a universal claim to truth. They naively believed their worldview derived from self-evident facts of human existence.

The difficulty people often have in recognizing their own religious presuppositions is evident in the debate between Hughes and Ketchum before the Common Council. The Bishop argued that it is impossible for one group to teach a common moral education ("essentials of religion") without offending the beliefs of some other group because groups will always differ regarding what moral education should be. But Ketchum could not comprehend this argument. Like Jefferson before him, and Mann in his own day, he sincerely believed that it was possible to foster universal moral training in a nonsectarian and nonoffensive way. And, as he stated before the Council, the Public School Society had the "right to declare moral truths."

The right, Ketchum admitted, comes not from the law but from the community. In the end Ketchum's definiton of religion prevailed because majoritarian "public sentiment" supported the Society's viewpoint. The Common Council rejected the Catholic petition, and the Society continued to receive all the money from the common school fund to support its schools.

Bishop Hughes was certainly disappointed by the Council's decision, but he was neither surprised nor defeated. He realized that the Catholic community had merely lost a skirmish in what was likely to be a long struggle for the "claims of justice and equal rights." Addressing his fellow Catholics, he pointed out the only question that really had to be addressed:

> What, then, remains for us to do? We must not fold our arms and rest. We must take measures. . . . I trust that no such defeat as we have experienced—the defeat of justice by authority—shall make you give up your principles. Spread it abroad that you ask no favor . . . but that you have rights and these rights you claim. Let them reserve their favors for those who want them. This is the ground on which the question will meet with respect, both from your brethren in faith, and your fellow-citizens at large. This is a question of right; and though a whole Board should be found to bend

---

Jefferson's Religious Views and Their Significance on the Supreme Court's Interpretation of the First Amendment," *Catholic University Law Review*, 26 [Fall 1976]: 64).

the knee to the Baal of bigotry, men will be found who can stand unawed in its presence, and do right.[15]

John C. Spencer, the New York secretary of state, was just such a person. He was concerned with the demands of both the law and justice. Acting in his capacity as ex officio superintendent of public schools, he submitted in 1841 an official report to the state senate, which became embroiled in the New York City educational struggle. Spencer agreed with Governor Seward that there was a legitimate state interest in providing for the education of all children in the state, because citizens must be educated if they are to participate in the democratic process. But he was also concerned that the state's interest should be met in a way that did not sacrifice the rights of any individual or group in society. In examining the Catholic claim that justice demanded they receive a proportional share of public funds for their schools, he expressed his concern this way:

> It can scarcely be necessary to say that the founders of these schools, and those who wish to establish others, have absolute rights to the benefits of a common burthen; and that any system which deprives them of their just share in application of a common and public fund, must be justified, if at all, by a necessity which demands the sacrifice of individual rights, for the accomplishment of a social benefit of paramount importance. It is presumed no such necessity can be urged in the present instance.[16]

The secretary of state responded to those who assumed that education could be nonsectarian by pointing out that "No books can be found, no reading lessons can be selected, which do not contain more or less of some principles of religious faith, either directly avowed, or indirectly assumed," and he proceeded to apply the point directly to the activities of the Public School Society:

> Even the moderate degree of religious instruction which the Public School Society imparts, must therefore be sectarian; that is, it must favor one set of opinions in opposition to another, or others;

---

15. Hughes, quoted by Lannie in *Public Money and Parochial Eduation*, p. 78.

16. "Report of the Secretary of State upon Memorials from the City of New-York, Respecting the Distribution of the Common School Moneys in That City, Referred to Him by the Senate, Document No. 86," *Documents of the Senate*, April 26, 1841, p. 6.

and it is believed that this always will be the result, in any course of education that the wit of man can devise.[17]

As if to anticipate the modern argument about the possibility of secular (neutral) education, Spencer pointed out that it was impossible to avoid sectarianism by abolishing religious instruction altogether:

> On the contrary, it would be in itself sectarian; because it would be consonant to the views of a peculiar class, and opposed to the opinions of other classes. Those who reject creeds and resist all efforts to infuse them into the minds of the young before they have arrived at a maturity of judgment which may enable them to form their own opinions, would be gratified by a system which so fully accomplishes their purposes. But there are those who hold contrary opinions; and who insist on guarding the young against the influences of their own passions, and the contagion of vice, by implanting in their minds and hearts, those elements of faith which are held by this class to be the indispensable foundations of moral principles. This description of persons regard neutrality and indifference as the most insidious forms of hostility. It is not the business of the undersigned [John C. Spencer] to express any opinion on the merits of these views. His only purpose is to show the mistake of those who suppose they may avoid sectarianism by avoiding all religious instruction.[18]

Spencer went to the heart of the educational controversy by pointing out that calling something nonsectarian does not make it so.[19] What is

---

17. "Report of the Secretary of State," pp. 9-10.
18. "Report of the Secretary of State," p. 13. At another point the Secretary of State refers to the neutral or secular argument as a "sectarian principle" (p. 12). As pointed out in Charles Glenn's paper (pp. 25-56 herein), this same insight into the impossibility of nonsectarian or neutral education is what led a Committee on Education of the House of Representatives in Massachusetts one year earlier (1840) to criticize the monopolist system of public education established by Horace Mann. The House committee challenged Mann's assumption that education could avoid feelings of jealousy by being neutral toward all perspectives. In addition, the committee pointed out that even if neutrality was possible in education (which it denied), it was not desirable, because a book "containing no party or sectarian views, will be likely to leave the mind in a state of doubt and skepticism, much more to be deplored than any party or sectarian bias" ("Report of the Committee on Education of the House of Representatives, March 7, 1840," reprinted in Welter, *American Writings*, p. 92).
19. In the educational controversy of the 1840s, the term *secular* was a synonym for *nonsectarian*. It was used, for example, in the Public School Society's defense of its educational perspective before the Common Council. "We

nonsectarian to one group is often seen as sectarian by another. Because by its very nature education always reflects different views of life and different understandings of moral training, it cannot hope to avoid religious issues.

The question that Spencer faced was how to do justice to different views in the allocation of public funds to schools. He concluded that justice demands the recognition "of the choice of parents" in the education of their children.[20] The only way this would be possible, he believed, was through an evenhanded distribution of public funds to all schools, regardless of their perspectives on education.[21]

Spencer did not convince the New York State legislature of the justice of this position. In the face of the growing anti-Catholic sentiment of the Nativist movement, any hope that a Protestant majority would approve educational funds going to a Catholic minority was out

---

have the right to declare moral truths.... We thus undertake in these public schools to furnish this secular education, embracing as it does, not solely and exclusively the common rudiments of learning, but also a knowledge of good morals, and those common sanctions of religion which are acknowledged by every body" (quoted by Lannie in *Public Money and Parochial Education*, p. 83). Years later the concept of secular education would be championed by secularists who assumed education could be nonreligious but who were themselves deeply religious in their secular worldview.

20. Document No. 86, *Documents of the Senate*, April 26, 1841, p. 11. Spencer was critical of the Public School Society because "It provides an educational establishment, and solicits the charge of children to be placed under its exclusive control, without allowing to the parents of the pupil the direction of the course of studies, the management of the schools, or any voice in the selection of teachers; it calls for no action or co-operation on the part of these parents, other than the entire submission of their children to the government and guidance of others, probably strangers, and who are in no way accountable to these parents. Such a system is so foreign to the feelings, habits and usages of our citizens, that its failure to enlist their confidence, and induce a desire to place their children under its control, ought not to excite surprise" (p. 19).

21. To illustrate his proposal, the secretary of state compared a monopolist structure for schools "to the religious establishments formed and supported by the governments of Europe, upon the plea that they are necessary to the moral instruction of the people; and that without them, their subjects would degenerate into heathenism. It was reserved for the American people to prove the fallacy of this position. An experience of fifty years has shown that religious worship has been better provided for, and attendance upon it has been more general, by being left to the free and voluntary action of the people, without the aid of any legal establishment; in other words, without any attempt to coerce the support of religious institutions, or to compel any one to participate in their advantages" (Document No. 86, *Documents of the Senate*, April 26, 1841, pp. 18-19).

of the question. The best that could be accomplished was for the city to take over the schools of the Public School Society and place them under the supervision of an elected board of education and state superintendent of public schools.

The structural consequences of this political development meant the formalization of a clean line of separation between public and private schools. The change, however, was not that radical. In reality it simply meant that the nongovernment monopolist structure of the Public School Society was replaced by the government monopolist structure of a public school establishment. The real significance in the educational controversies of the 1820s and 1840s was the transformation of New York City's original pluralist funding policy into a monopolist policy similar to that in Massachusetts and to the policies that were developing in other parts of the country.

There is little question that there was a pressing need in cities such as New York and elsewhere for more educational opportunities. Academies, church schools, and charity schools were not adequately meeting the needs of an increasing school population. Expanding educational opportunities, however, did not have to come by way of a monopolist public school establishment. It is conceivable that the principle of proportional funding to a diversity of schools could have been expanded to meet the increasing educational challenge. This was the recommendation of both Governor Seward and Secretary of State Spencer. The fact that this course of action was not followed is an indication of how public policy is often shaped by self-serving political and ideological choices of majoritarian interests rather than by a self-conscious understanding of the demands of public justice for all citizens.

Thus far I have argued that the modern meaning of public education clearly reflects nineteenth-century political and ideological choices. Majoritarian interest often intentionally created a nonpluralist educational monopoly in order to exclude minorities from receiving public funds for their schools. Today a clean line of separation between public and private schools is deeply rooted in American society. But the public school establishment is now facing a crisis of legitimacy. The roots of a good part of the crisis can be traced directly to unresolved tensions inherent in the monopolist structure of the nineteenth-century educational establishment.

THE TWENTIETH CENTURY: THE CRISIS OF LEGITIMACY

As I noted at the outset of this essay, a recent wave of reports and studies of American schools indicates that education in America is facing many serious problems. The National Commission on Excellence in Education opened its report, A *Nation at Risk*, with the now familiar warning that "the educational foundations of our society are presently being eroded by a rising tide of mediocrity."

State boards of education and legislatures, local school boards, and colleges and universities have been awakened to the educational crisis. Some states are already raising teachers' salaries, and schools are making new attempts to measure "quality" and improve their curricular offerings.

But more money and improved educational offerings will not resolve all the problems facing American education, especially when it comes to the controversial issue of "values education." I am convinced that in this controversy the very legitimacy of public education as it is presently defined and structured is being called into question.

This crisis of legitimacy can be traced in part to the fact that we live today in a post-Enlightenment age. There is evidence for this development in the involvement of parents, teachers, and administrators in the current controversy over values education and in the "post-empiricist" rejection of the idea of value-free knowledge. Since Richard Baer's essay discusses this latter point (see pp. 1-24 herein), I will focus primarily on the former.[22]

In the early nineteenth century, even Enlightenment figures such as Jefferson and Mann did not believe that public education could be separated from the common religion (universal moral precepts) of society. By the twentieth century, however, the commitment to nonsectarian education was transformed into a commitment to *secular* education.[23] With this development, secular education and public edu-

---

22. I would simply add here that the "post-empiricist" rejection of the ideal of value-free education is an important contemporary development. More and more scholars are coming to realize that it is impossible to avoid religious issues in education. Even to choose to avoid any discussion of ultimate questions in science, history, and literature is to assert that these disciplines can be taught while ignoring religion. This judgment is itself a religious viewpoint. See Richard John Neuhaus, "No More Bootleg Religion," in *Controversies in Education*, ed. Dwight W. Allen and Jeffry C. Hecht (Philadelphia: W. B. Sounders, 1974). For an insightful overview of the post-empiricist rejection of value-free knowledge, see David Lyon, "Valuing in Social Science: Post-Empiricism and Christian Response," *Christian Scholars Review* 12 (1983).

23. In a discussion that like so many is often complicated by the variety of semantic twists given to key terms, the etymology of *secular* is particularly ironic. The word derives from the Latin *saeculum*, meaning "a generation, age." It

cation became synonymous. In the twentieth century a secular-religious disjunction became central to the modern definition of public education and to the political and legal justification for the exclusive (nonpluralist) public funding of a monopolist educational establishment at the elementary and secondary levels.

We have seen how the conflict over "values education" in the early nineteenth century helped to create a monopolist educational establishment. Bishop Hughes and Catholic parents argued in the 1840s that public schools undermined Catholic family views. This argument was not accepted by the majority of New Yorkers because early on they sincerely believed that education could be nonsectarian, and later they came to believe that education could be secular. They believed, on either nonsectarian or secular grounds, that a monopolist system of education could legitimately serve the needs of all citizens in the city.

One of the results of the modern conflict over values education is that more parents, teachers, and administrators are being forced to discuss whether or not secular education is in fact possible—and if so, what the effects on students and on the society as a whole might be if education is conceived as no more that the teaching of facts and mechanical skills. The debate is making it clearer to many people that if secular or value-free education is not possible, then a monopolist system of public education cannot legitimately serve the needs of a pluralist society.

The recent educational controversy in Arlington, Virginia, is a case in point. The dispute arose when eleventh grade American history students read and discussed "Alligator River," an allegorical tale in which "a young woman must decide whether to sleep with the captain of a boat in exchange for a ride across the river to see her lover."[24] The classroom teacher defended the use of the story because "it provided an excellent way to get the students to discover how people have to negotiate when they must make painful and difficult choices." Some parents, however, objected to what they saw as the disturbing moral implications of the story and its use in the classroom. At the heart of the Arlington

---

was used to describe things that occurred only once in a great while—notably the "secular games" of ancient Rome, which were held in honor of the gods. These events combined athletic competition with dramatic presentations, hymns, and sacrifices. As an adjective describing the games, *secular* thus developed some pointedly religious connotations. In modern English usage, of course, the meaning is precisely the opposite. Those who advocate secular education typically champion the empiricist ideal of value-free (which is to say, specifically nonreligious) education.

24. For an account of the situation, see the *Washington Post*, 6 February, 1985, p. 1.

debate is a basic philosophical rift about values and their interpretation.

In the Arlington controversy, teachers as well as parents are caught in a dilemma created by the fact that one public school system attempts to serve the diversity of views that exist in the public community. Marjorie McCreery, executive director of the Arlington Education Association, points out that in highly diverse communities such as Arlington it is important to encourage critical thinking and questioning in order to help students live together. "You can't avoid values." But if values cannot be avoided, neither can the controversy that erupts when a monopolist structure is confronted by the reality of a diversity of deeply held values and beliefs.

What is significant in the "Alligator River" dispute and in many similar incidents throughout the country is the fact that the debate is no longer limited to specific classroom material. As Dorthy Massie, a National Education Association staff member has stated, "There's no question that there is much more of a general trend of parent protest not against specific books but against the whole direction of a curriculum." It is becoming more evident to participants on all sides of the values education controversy that what is at stake is a basic disagreement over the way different worldviews shape a curriculum and the very life of an educational institution.

We would do well to remember that a clash of worldviews was at the heart of the schoolbook controversy between Catholics and the Public School Society in the 1840s. While the debate often centered on specific books or passages, it was clear to Catholics that the conflict went much deeper. Though representatives of the Society tried on occasion to remove some of the more offensive material, they never fully comprehended Bishop Hughes's fundamental objection to instruction that he believed implicitly reflected a Protestant worldview. Furthermore, Hughes realized that if offending material could be removed one year it could be reinstated at another time. On one occasion this is exactly what happened. The issue for Catholics, therefore, was not so much specific objectionable material as it was the monopolist educational structure that led to one perspective defining the type of education that was available to all students in the public schools. It was impossible, Catholics concluded, for a monopolist structure such as the Public School Society to accommodate a diversity of perspectives. Many people are reaching the same conclusion today concerning values education in a monopolist educational system.

There is a significant difference between the 1840s situation in New York and our situation today, however. In the 1840s debate, the

Catholics constituted a minority. Today there is evidence to indicate that support for "traditional values" is still strong in many communities and that a *majority* of Americans currently feel that their perspective is being compromised or even excluded from public school instruction.

But in a larger sense, the question of whether it is a majority or a minority that is dissatisfied is not of first importance. The the real issue is that in a pluralist society, there is little possibility that a "public" monopolist structure will be able to accommodate or reflect the different perspectives and values that inevitably exist within the "public" community. In the case of a monopolist educational establishment, one group or a coalition of groups usually gains the upper hand, claims the title "public," and forces "the others" either to compromise their principles to remain in the system or to leave and pay a second time for education that is not offensive to their deeply held beliefs.

Not too long ago there was an educational controversy in New York that was reminiscent of the earlier conflict between Bishop Hughes and the Public School Society. As we have seen, the monopolist structure of the Public School Society was merely replaced in the 1840s by the monopolist structure of a government-run public school establishment. In the late 1970s this monopolist structure produced another "battle of the textbooks" when the Nassau chapter of the New York Civil Liberties Union filed a lawsuit against the Island Trees school district to block censorship of books by its school board. In announcing the lawsuit, the executive director of the Nassau chapter of the NYCLU wrote, "The students and teachers . . . have a right to read and to discuss thoughts unhampered by the state or by the fears of individuals representing the state."[25]

In response, a reader asked how this freedom could "be achieved in a public school, which is itself an instrument of the state." The questioner went on to say,

> The State school system imposes on its captive audience, or at least continually exposes that captive audience to, the values (literary, historical, social) that the system believes should be imposed. How can we justify this kind of situation where "an individual representing the state" is really in control of the thought processes of supposedly free American citizens? Is a state es-

---

25. This and following quotations are taken from the March-April 1977 issue of *N.Y. Civil Liberties*, which is published by the New York Civil Liberties Union.

tablishment of education any more tolerable than a state establishment of religion?

It is not the actions of an isolated public school board, but the whole public school system, that NYCLU should re-examine. If NYCLU is concerned about the suppression of freedom in the schools, why not strike at the root of the problem instead of making such a big fuss about pruning away a few branches here and there now and then?

Ira Glasser, then executive director of the New York Chapter of the American Civil Liberties Union, admitted that neither the NYCLU nor the national organization had yet come to grips with this basic anomaly in their position. Glasser clearly indicated that the tension between freedom and control was intrinsic to Jefferson's educational views and the very system of public education he envisioned:

> From its inception, the notion of public education for a democratic citizenry has contained within it a tension between freedom of thought and control of curriculum. Of course, the public schools have usually accomplished their goals less through blunt censorship and more through "judicious choice of required texts and the careful appointment" of teachers. The criteria involved in these decisions are rarely obvious, and frequently involve differences sufficiently subtle to defy clear perception. The great battles over censorship or academic freedom have usually occurred when a mistake was made: the wrong book slipped through or the wrong teacher hired. The school's effort to undo such mistakes makes explicit the political criteria of their routine decisions. But if the mistakes are not made, if the celebrated incident is avoided, the political criteria usually remain invisible.

If we add other value judgments to "political criteria," the difficulty a monopolist educational system experiences in attempting to accommodate the diversity of views represented in the public community becomes even clearer. Glasser ended his search for a solution to the anomaly not with an answer but by returning to the question that is inherent in the very structure of a public school establishment: "On the one hand, schools claim to transmit the culture of diversity and the habits of free inquiry. But in their every decisions, they necessarily reflect majoritarian views, or the views of the particular majority that happens to control a particular school. How can that necessary conflict be resolved?"

In a curious way this question is not unlike the question another

New Yorker asked when confronted with majoritarian sentiments that denied his people a full measure of educational freedom and choice in a democratic society. Bishop Hughes's question is as relevant today as when he first asked it: "What, then, remains for us to do?" The need for an answer presses on all people who are genuinely concerned with human rights.

The New York City educational controversy in the 1840s, the Island Trees conflict in the 1970s, and the recent Arlington dispute are not unique; they are representative of a long list of conflicts that highlight the tension inherent in a monopolist educational establishment. Today no consensus exists concerning the modern equation of secular and public education or the appropriateness of one educational system claiming the title of public when in fact it cannot serve all the groups that make up the public community. This point was recently made quite forcefully by Secretary of Education William Bennett when he declared that

> In a pluralistic society such as our own—the most gloriously diverse the world has ever seen—that right and high duty [of parents to nurture their children] is no longer compatible with government monopoly in schooling. It is no longer possible for us to assume that neighbors will share the same vision of the truth just because they live on the same city block. It is no longer conceivable that feminists, fundamentalists, and every other group will somehow come to agree with each other on how to handle sex education, or dress codes, or whether to begin the day with a prayer. The whole point of being Americans is that we do not have to agree. Except for a few precious principles, there is no official orthodoxy in this country, and that is precisely the reason why many of our ancestors came here to begin with.[26]

In the controversy over values education there is a growing recognition that education is inherently value-laden. "All education," as T. S. Eliot has said, "is religious education." This realization is in turn leading to fundamental questions regarding the legitimacy of both the modern (secular) definition and the monopolist structure of public education. We are coming to see that we live in a post-Enlightenment age in which a monopolist educational establishment cannot meet the educational needs of a pluralist society.

---

26. Bennett, speaking before the National Catholic Education Association Annual Convention, St. Louis, Missouri, 10 April 1985.

THE FUTURE: TOWARD GENUINE EDUCATIONAL PLURALISM AND DISESTABLISHMENT

Our society is facing a number of unresolved educational issues. The matter of values education is certainly one of the most difficult to resolve within the present monopolist structure of public education. Without a doubt we are living in a period that will see significant changes in American education. At this point I would simply ask with Bishop Hughes, "What, then, remains for us to do?" I propose five steps, not as a fully developed response to this question but as initial suggestions about what needs to be done now and in the future.[27]

Step One. In order to promote greater justice for schools in the United States, we must recognize the need for a more pluralist view of the state. State unity is important, but it is counterproductive to attempt to build it through a public school establishment. Rather, it must grow as a public legal unity that recognizes the spiritual, moral, and intellectual diversity that exists among its citizens.[28]

The opening words of the preamble to the Constitution read "We the people of the United States, in order to form a more perfect union, establish justice. . . ." This close linking of political unity with justice is a clear testimony that the framers felt the new country had to be based on the rule of law, not on common descent, language, or religion. In the field of education I believe the rule of law and justice for all citizens demands the nondiscriminatory allocation of educational resources to all citizens.

The process by which the church was disestablished in America ought to be followed now in the realm of education. The school must be freed from a monopolist establishment. This does not mean that it would be necessary to prohibit the state from running any school system whatsoever; the only requirement is that true equity, proportional justice, should be instituted for all schools. In other words, funding provisions and all other public legal measures must be

---

27. The five steps were initially set forth in McCarthy, et al., *Disestablishment a Second Time*, pp. 124-36. Strategies for change are discussed more fully in McCarthy, et al., *Society, State, and Schools*, pp. 169-208.

28. For a fuller discussion of what stands behind the concept of a "public legal unity," see my essay "American Civil Religion," in *Confessing Christ and Doing Politics* (Washington: APJ Education Fund, 1982); and James Skillen's "Societal Pluralism: Blessing or Curse for the Public Good," in *The Ethical Dimension of Political Life: Essays in Honor of John H. Hollowell*, ed. Francis Canavan, (Durham, N.C.: Duke University Press, 1983).

nondiscriminatory. No favor or penalty should be directed toward any particular school or school system. Ideally, a state-owned and -operated school should be one among many that are recognized as public schools by the government.[29]

Some might object that I am outlining the principle of *multiple establishment*, and that this approach was rejected in Virginia and elsewhere when it was first offered as an alternative to a monopolist church-state establishment. It is true that every form of ecclesiastical establishment was rejected in Virginia and eventually elsewhere as well. This was the direct result of the judgment that compulsory financial support and compulsory attendance were not consistent with the norm of justice for all. In reference to education, however, it is widely accepted today that it is just for everyone to be taxed for the support of schools and for every child to be required by law to be educated (for most this means attending school) for a number of years. Given these two democratic judgments about education, it is clear that reasons for rejecting a multiple church-state establishment (compulsory financing and attendance) are not relevant to a consideration of multiple support for a variety of different kinds of public schools.

Step Two. To promote greater public justice for schools, we must redefine the nature of public responsibility for education. Recognizing pluralism in education and disestablishing the state's public school monopoly will broaden the definition of a legitimate public school. Once the state school is disestablished, the present distinction between "public" privileged schools and "private" unsupported schools will come to an end. An important question will then be "What is a public school?"

At the elementary and secondary level in the present system this question is not raised because, by definition, a public school is whatever the local governments and state boards of education have established as a school. But once the state loses its privilege of establishing the "definition" of a public school by virtue of its authority to establish a monopolist school system, criteria will have to be set to distinguish between schools that truly qualify as public schools and those that do not.

Public justice for all demands that every school that meets accreditation standards be recognized as serving a public purpose and thus deserving a proportional share of public funds. It is certain that some schools will always want to remain private institutions. This status

---

29. On this, see, for example, Richard John Neuhaus, "Educational Diversity in Post-Secular America," *New York University Education Quarterly*, Winter 1982; and Donald A. Erickson, *The New "Public" Schools* (Wichita: Center for Independent Education, 1977).

would obviously make such schools ineligible for public funds. The freedom of choice, the freedom to be a private school, must be protected.

It is quite another thing, however, for a fully accredited school to be forced outside the public community simply because some have judged its educational philosophy to be unworthy of public support. In order to make this point as clear and forceful as possible, the term "private school" ought to be reserved for those institutions that either do not want to be considered public schools or that do not measure up to the standards established for a public school. The term "public school" would then describe the diversity of schools that meet all accreditation standards and desire a proportional share of public funds for education. In such a case, the label "public" would attest to a school's service to society rather than indicating that it was owned and operated by the government.

Clearly, then, a pluralist reform of education along these lines would not entail the destruction of public education in the United States. It would simply entail the recognition of a greater diversity of schools worthy of public support. Such a reform would require a redefinition of public responsibility for education, however, and this in turn would require new and better accreditation procedures. Several resources could facilitate this task.

First, there is the definition of public education that existed in the United States prior to the 1840s. A broader, more pluralist definition of public education is available within our own history. While no one is foolish enough to suggest that this country ought to return to all the educational practices of our early history, it would also be foolish to ignore valuable lessons from history that point the way toward a more normative understanding of public education.

Second, the actual educational practices in some states today reflect this country's original, more pluralist understanding of public education. What I have in mind are examples from several New England states in which public funds are used to support a variety of schools.

Joe Nathan has reported that in Maine more than thirty towns without high schools of their own allow their students to attend any of several public, private, or parochial high schools, with the town paying their tuition. In Vermont for more than one hundred years the state has used tax funds to support payment of tuition at different types of schools. According to Nathan,

There are four broad classes of schools in Vermont: public

schools which meet all state requirements; private schools designated public schools in towns which have not established their own school; private, nonsectarian schools which meet certain state requirements (less stringent than the first two groups of schools); and finally, private schools associated with religious groups (principally the Catholic church).[30]

Of the 246 towns in Vermont, 95 allow families to use tax funds to attend a variety of schools, including private nonsectarian institutions. The regulations established to define the educational program (curriculum, staff, buildings, and schedule) of Vermont schools are a resource that can inform the accreditation procedures for a more pluralist educational system.

Maine's and Vermont's experience with freedom of choice in education demonstrates that such a program can work without destroying the public schools or the fabric of society—two claims often made about the effects of a more pluralist view of education. These examples ought to be more carefully analyzed to determine levels of student, parent, and community satisfaction. In addition, other states ought to be studied for more examples of workable models of educational pluralism.

A third resource that can help to create new and better accreditation procedures is the precedent of pluralist educational achievements in Canadian provinces and European states.[31] By examining their policies we can gain valuable insights into how governments recognize a plurality of schools and school systems without supporting fraudulent, illegitimate, or racist institutions.

And fourth, we have in this country at the present time a highly diverse system of higher education. Among colleges and universities (and even among some preparatory high schools), sophisticated accrediting institutions and procedures demonstrate the power and ability that schools have for independent and critical self-evaluation.

By carefully considering American educational history, educational practices of some American states and other democratic countries, and contemporary higher education accreditation procedures in this country, we can develop criteria and procedures for schools and school systems to qualify as voucher, tax-credit, or tax-

---

30. Joe Nathan, *Free to Teach: Achieving Equity and Excellence in Schools* (Minneapolis: Winston Press, 1984), p. 145.
31. On this, see McCarthy, et al., *Disestablishment a Second Time*, pp. 107-23; and *Society, State, and Schools*, pp. 136-44. See also *Consociational Democracy: Political Accommodation in Segmented Societies*, ed. Kenneth McRae (Toronto: McClelland & Stewart, 1974).

deduction schools for parents and students. It is extremely important in the development of criteria and procedures for public recognition that there be no interference in the educational philosophy of the diverse schools. If a variety of schools is to be encouraged and sustained, then the state or a nongovernment accrediting association must not be allowed to dictate the perspective of those schools under its authority. It is one thing, for example, to require English language competency and the teaching of American history and government. These and many more legitimate requirements are necessary for minimum competency and citizen participation in a democratic society. It is something quite different for an accrediting body to dictate the educational philosophy that must guide the teaching of the social or natural sciences. But again, this should not be an insurmountable problem. It has been effectively dealt with by accredited institutions of higher learning in this country.

Taking the second step of redefining the nature of public responsibility for education will end the decades-old struggle to define what is "secular" and what is "religious" in education. If schools are freed from inclusion in or exclusion from the state monopoly, then the secular/religious distinction will be irrelevant because a school will not have to claim some privileged identity (as "nonsectarian" or "secular") in order to allow parents and students to obtain public funds for education. Then the courts and other public institutions will be able to concentrate their energies on the proper public legal issues of determining what true equity demands for education and deciding what proportional justice demands for a variety of schools and school systems. And the government will be encouraged to assume its full responsibility for nurturing good citizens without having to control and favor a monopolist school system to the unjust disadvantage of other schools.

Step Three. To ensure justice for schools, the government must give greater recognition to parental responsibility and freedom of choice in the matter of the education of children. If a true diversity of schools is encouraged on the basis of the first two steps outlined above, that in itself will be a major step toward helping parents fulfill their responsibility to educate their children. But even if the government turns over the duties of serving as the legal "principle" and "agent" in education to parents and schools, it will still have to shape public policy. For example, what will justice require for parents who cannot find a school that meets the needs of their children within the local community? What extra consideration will have to be given to financing the education of children who are handicapped, who have learning disabilities, who come from families living in poverty? What is equitable for those who have suffered racial or other forms of discrimination?

It is vitally important that government recognize the nature and the identity of family life and its relationship to the training of children. Since children are not merely citizens, and except for unusual circumstances, certainly not wards of the state, their life in families must be recognized and nurtured in a way that harmonizes formal school education with family life.

Step Four. To promote justice for American schools, state and federal governments must encourage the development of new schools by clarifying the rights, privileges, and responsibilities of founding organizations and cooperating institutions.[32] Once the government no longer grants a monopoly of public funds to a single school system, new schools will be able to open and older nongovernment schools will gain strength. Many churches are likely to remain in (or enter) the educational field. Independent associations of parents will continue to establish schools. Business enterprises and other organizations will establish new schools.[33] And local and state governments are certain to keep the government schools alive.

All of this can become a very healthy, liberating process, encouraging the infusion of new energy into creative educational ventures. A diversity of schools will promote a rethinking of American economic, social, political, and religious life. Such a diversity will be healthful for the republic as a whole. In the end it will lead to a greater public awareness of the rule of law and democratic values than is presently possible under a monopolist educational structure that denies freedom of choice in education to millions of students.

---

32. For a discussion of the "rights of associations," see McCarthy, et al., *Society, State, and Schools*, pp. 51-78; and my essays "Liberal Democracy and the Rights of Institutions" (*Pro Rege*, June 1980) and "Three Societal Models: A Theoretical and Historical Overview" (*Pro Rege*, June 1981).

33. The scope of corporate education in the United States already rivals traditional programs. According to a report by Nell Eurich, a Carnegie Foundation trustee, "nearly $60 billion a year is spent on corporate education, making it 'similar to the cost of the nation's four-year colleges and universities, both public and private.' In addition, the number of employees enrolled in corporate programs is close to the total enrollment of colleges and universities—about eight million students. Eurich found at least 18 corporations awarding academic degrees. These corporations are or soon will be accredited. The Rand Corporation offers a Ph.D., for example, and Wang Laboratories in Massachusetts offers a master of computer software" ("Corpo-

This fourth step will require some gradual redesign of public funding procedures and of the legal identity of schools and their supporting organizations, but changes can be made gradually through new state and federal legislation, state constitutional amendments, and court decisions on various contested issues. The changes do not require the sudden, destructive overthrow of the present order.

Step Five. If we take these four steps, it will be possible to take a fifth step. If public schools are freed in this way to be schools instead of branches of government bureaucracies, they will have an incentive to dedicate themselves to excellence in education. School administrators will be freer to offer their services to the schools they choose rather than to the only available establishment. Teachers will be free to look for school communities in which they can share similar interests with colleagues rather than having to settle for working side by side with teachers who are committed to a different educational philosophy or a different view of the educational process. Students will be free to participate in schools that reflect some degree of harmony with their family lives. They will have a variety of educational reasons for attending a particular school rather than being forced by arbitrary geographical reasons to attend the only available local government school. Parent-teacher associations will be genuine associations based on common and freely chosen commitments rather than on accidental and compulsory geographical and political factors.

Schools that do not offer a good educational program will be forced out of existence by competiton, because parents will not have to continue sending their children to them. Excellence will breed further excellence. Educational reforms and improvements will arise through the natural quest for excellence in dozens of different schools and school systems rather than from the top down to a captive and therefore often passive audience.

If we take these five steps, we can realistically anticipate a greater measure of public justice, public responsibility for education, parental dedication, school growth, educational excellence, and much more.

CONCLUSION

Not everyone will agree that a more pluralist and equitable system of public funding for schools will improve education and create a more

---

rate Classrooms: The Learning Business," *Higher Education and National Affairs*, March 1985).

democratic society. While increasing numbers of individuals and groups have become critical of the present monopolist system of public education, others are rallying to its defense. In the minds and hearts of many citizens, public officials, and scholars, the present public school establishment is the only conceivable structure for a democratic society. At this juncture in our history the political-educational debate will continue on many fronts between those who are committed to maintaining the present monopolist establishment and those who believe that public justice demands disestablishing the present monopoly and replacing it with a pluralist system of education.

If we return to the argument that the closest analogy to the present public school establishment in our country is the state-church establishment of former days, then a number of things come into focus. First, as recently as the eighteenth century in America most people assumed that one of the primary functions of an established church was to *enforce* a common morality. They viewed an ecclesiastical establishment as crucial to the very survival of society.

Those first Americans who objected to the state-church establishment found it difficult to oppose because no society had as yet disestablished the church. When disestablishment finally did occur, people saw that a democratic society could indeed survive without one church or a number of churches having a favored political status.

Was it the case, however, that with the disestablishment of the church, America freed itself from the assumption that a common morality was to be enforced in society? Many think not. John F. Wilson, for example, believes that an established public school simply replaced an established church as the mechanism to enforce a common morality:

> The public school system certainly must be viewed as a powerful engine for reinforcement of common religion.... School systems are in fact the American religious establishment through their state symbolism, civic ceremonial, inculcated values, exemplified virtues, and explicit curricula.[34]

Elwyn A. Smith concludes similarly that "the American public school system is the nation's equivalent to the European established church."[35]

---

34. Wilson, "The Status of 'Civil Religion' in America," in *The Religion of the Republic*, ed. Elwyn A. Smith (Philadelphia: Fortress Press, 1971), pp. 7, 8-9.

35. Smith, *The Religion of the Republic*, p. viii. The same point was made much earlier by Sidney E. Mead ("Thomas Jefferson's 'Fair

Today many individuals and groups believe that disestablishing the public school would threaten the survival of our society. Fortunately, unlike those who first objected to the former state-church establishment, we have today abundant evidence to demonstrate that democratic societies do not merely survive but flourish when a state recognizes a diversity of schools as legitimately fulfilling the task of educating young women and men for responsible citizenship. It is curious that while the United States pointed the way for other democratic states to disestablish the church, it finds itself today one of the few democratic countries in which a monopolist education establishment is still maintained.

A second lesson to be learned from viewing the present educational establishment in the light of an older state-church establishment is that people protested for many years before others recognized the injustice of an ecclesiastical establishment. In time a broad coalition of people and groups did appear and eventually change did occur.

Where, we might ask, are we today in relationship to the same type of social, economic, religious, and political forces that eventually brought down the state church establishment? That these forces are at work in contemporary American society and that opposition groups and coalitions are emerging should be clear to all. I am convinced that eventually this process will significantly reform the structure of American education.

There is, however, no single best method for bringing about change; there are several roads, but no single clearly preferable road, to reform the structure of public education in America. The educational framework that now exists is an intricate interrelationship of local, state, and federal responsibility and control. No single point of attack can change such a complex educational establishment. Instead we must seek change through new state and federal legislation; through local, particularly urban, reforms that can become models for other communities; through the courts; through amendments to state and the federal constitution; through consciousness-raising; and through other processes as well.

The movement toward genuine educational pluralism and disestablishment will require many different kinds of cooperative efforts made by many individuals and groups. Bishop Hughes's question is still very relevant: "What, then, remains for us to do?" Academic, political,

---

Experiment'—Religious Freedom," in *The Lively Experiment: The Shaping of Christianity in America* [New York: Harper & Row, 1963], p. 68).

and other strategists must continue to bring their most creative insights to bear on this question and the issue of the relationship between public education and public justice in a pluralistic society.

Changing Assumptions in the Public Governance of Education: What Has Changed and What Ought to Change

James W. Skillen

Education in the United States has been shaped by public policies emerging from a number of fundamental assumptions. At least two of those assumptions are fundamentally incompatible, and the contradictions and dilemmas caused by that incompatibility are becoming increasingly apparent.

The first of these assumptions has its roots deep in Greek and Roman traditions that were revived in the West during the Renaissance and the Enlightenment. Its ruling principle is that the government of a city or state holds the primary and direct responsibility for educating its citizens. To whatever extent government recognizes the authority of other institutions (such as families, independent associations, churches, etc.), those authorities are nonetheless viewed as subservient to government in the area of education.[1]

The second assumption, which is rooted in the biblical tradition of ancient Judaism and Christianity and in aspects of Roman culture, recognizes the primacy of parental authority in the education of children. Some governmental responsibility for schooling may be

---

1. On this, see H. I. Marrou, *A History of Education in Antiquity*, trans. George Lamb (New York: Mentor Books, 1956), pp. xi-xii, 41-42, 77-78, 147-53, 315-17, 325-41, 400-418; Fustelde Coulanges, *The Ancient City: A Study on the Religion, Laws and Institutions of Greece and Rome* (Garden City, N.Y.: Doubleday, 1956); and Frederick Eby and Charles Flinn Arrowwood, *The History and Philosophy of Education Ancient and Modern* (New York: Prentice-Hall, 1946).

legitimate, according to this tradition, and a variety of agencies outside the home may be required for the education of young people, but laws governing schooling must be built on respect for the primacy of the parental role in the education of children.[2]

Both of these assumptions have been operative throughout the development of American schooling. During the colonial period and up until about the 1840s, the second assumption was predominant. From the 1840s to the present, the first assumption has predominated. A tension between the two is still quite evident, because although we continue to hold onto both of them, it is not possible to act on both at the same time without contradiction and anomaly in law and public policy.

As it stands today, state and local governments (with federal and judicial support) assume the principal responsibility for public schooling and seek to fulfill that responsibility by means of their own state-established agencies—the common public schools.[3] Within this legal framework for education, the authority of parents over their children is incorporated into the general civic governing structure for the local public school: parents can exercise their responsibility with respect to their children's education through their membership in the political community, voting for school board members as well as for local, state, and federal officials. Parental principalship in education, in other words, is swallowed up in government principalship, and thus, by definition, public agencies (public schools) are treated as belonging to the parents by way of their citizenship.

Parents can also exercise their authority by removing their children from the public system of education and entrusting them to another agency of education—a nongovernment school, or perhaps

---

2. See Marrou, *History of Education*, pp. 313-20, 419- 38; Bruce C. Hafen, "The Constitutional Status of Marriage, Kinship, and Sexual Privacy—Balancing the Individual and Social Interests," *Michigan Law Review* 81 (January 1983): 570- 72; and Hafen, "Children's Liberation and the New Egalitarianism: Some Reservations about Abandoning Youth to Their 'Rights,'" *Brigham Young University Law Review* (1976): 613-19. For related court cases, see *Bellotti v. Baird*, 443 U.S. 622 (1979); *Meyer v. Nebraska*, 262 U.S. 390 (1923); and *Lochner v. New York*, 198 U.S. 45 (1905).

3. The terms *principal* and *agency* as I use them here have specific legal connotations regarding authority, accountability, and responsibility, especially in cases where minors, still under the authority of their parents, are involved in other agencies outside the home. A valuable article on this distinction, as it relates to education, was recently drawn to my attention, but I can no longer locate it in order to give proper credit to the author.

home schooling. This choice does not deprive parents of civic rights—they can continue to exercise responsibility in the public school arena, even serving on the local public school board, for example. Nor does the choice to opt out of the public school system relieve parents of the responsibility to pay taxes for the public schools. However, most people today label such a choice "private" and expect the parents who make it to undertake additional personal expense for the alternative education and also to give up many privileges attached to the public schools. The system removes parental primacy without eliminating parental initiative entirely.

To understand some of the contemporary problems caused by trying to operate in the context of these two competing assumptions, we will have to take an additional factor into account. Since the 1840s, Americans have arranged the priority of governmental primacy over parental primacy in education by identifying the first with what is "secular" while usually connecting the second with what is "religious."[4] This mode of identification is itself dependent on a modern Enlightenment viewpoint that is closely connected with the assumption that government has the principal responsibility for education. "Religion," in this frame of thought, is private, personal, and ecclesiastical. The "secular" is assumed to be the domain of the state, embracing all of the state's operations and institutions, including its schools.

The practical consequence of all this in our daily experience is that state and local governments in the United States since about the middle of the last century have assumed the prerogative of setting up and running schools for citizens on the grounds that they, the governments, are trustees of the secular public trust, which includes basic education. Parental (and other) authorities simply have to accept subservience to government's prior rights and responsibilities in this regard. If parents want to exercise the right to organize the education of their children directly, then by definition they must opt out of the public "secular" order in pursuit of a "private," frequently religious, course. And naturally a private or "religious" choice must be paid for by the private party, not by government.

This distinction between "private religion" and the "secular public" does not, however, properly clarify or substantiate the parental/governmental distinction. In fact, there is no necessary connection or overlap between these two distinctions except in the eyes of those who

---

4. See Diane Ravitch, *The Great School Wars: New York City, 1805-1973* (New York: Basic Books, 1974), pp. 3-76.

THE PUBLIC GOVERNANCE OF EDUCATION 89

hold a philosophy for which the connection is essential. The amalgamation of these distinctions only confuses matters, with the consequence that many states and the U.S. Supreme Court have been tied up for decades trying to resolve unresolvable dilemmas and contradictions in education laws. How much government aid can be channeled to the "secular" aspects of education in "private religious schools"? How much "religious" activity can be carried on within the public "secular" schools. How much freedom may parents and teachers exercise inside the public schools? What kind of "public" purpose is served by "private" schools? These questions have not yet been adequately answered by either the courts or the state legislatures.

I would like first to explore the public legal problems inherent in the framework of contemporary American schooling by trying to expose and analyze the dominant assumptions of governmental primacy and religious/secular stratification. Then I would like to suggest a way to change the assumptions and to overcome mistaken distinctions in order to resolve the contemporary dilemmas and contradictions in favor of greater justice for schools, families, and the larger civil society.

CONTINUITY AND CHANGE IN THE PRESENT ORDER OF EDUCATION

> Our decisions from *Everson* to *Allen* have permitted the States to provide church-related schools with secular, neutral, or nonideological services, facilities, or materials. Bus transportation, school lunches, public health services, and secular textbooks supplied in common to all students were not thought to offend the Establishment Clause.
>
> Chief Justice Warren Burger, *Lemon et al. v. Kurtzman*, 403 U.S. 602 (1971), pp. 616-17

Providing for the education of schoolchildren is surely a praiseworthy purpose. But our cases have consistently recognized that even such a praiseworthy, secular purpose cannot validate government aid to parochial schools when the aid has the effect of promoting a single religion or religion generally or when the aid unduly entangles the government in matters religious. For just as religion throughout history has provided spiritual comfort, guidance, and inspiration to many, it can also serve powerfully to divide societies and to exclude those whose beliefs are not in accord with particular religions or sects that have from time to time achieved dominance. The solution to this problem adopted by the Framers and consistently recognized by this Court is jealously

to guard the right of every individual to worship according to the dictates of conscience while requiring the government to maintain a course of neutrality among religions, and between religion and nonreligion.
> Justice William Brennan, *Grand Rapids School District of the City of Grand Rapids et al. v. Phyllis Ball et al.* (slip opinion of case Number 83-990, 1 July 1985, p. 8)

While the evolution of the public school system in this country marked an escape from denominational control and was therefore admirable as seen through the eyes of those who think like Madison and Jefferson, it had disadvantages. The main one is that a state system may attempt to mold all students alike according to views of the dominant group and to discourage the emergence of individual idiosyncrasies.
> Justice William O. Douglas, *Lemon et al. v. Kurtzman*, p. 630

The Court apparently believes that the Establishment Clause of the First Amendment not only mandates religious neutrality on the part of government but also requires that this Court go further and throw its weight on the side of those who believe that our society as a whole should be a purely secular one. Nothing in the First Amendment or in the cases interpreting it requires such an extreme approach to this difficult question.
> Justice William Rehnquist, *Meek et al. v. Pittenger*, 421 U.S. 349 (1975), p. 395

The decisions of the U.S. Supreme Court on school issues from the earliest to the most recent display a set of widely held assumptions clearly conveyed by the justices' use of the words *secular, religious, neutral, sectarian, nonsectarian, ideological, nonideological, church-related, public,* and *private*. The language of the Court's decisions is broadly representative of popular American thinking and speaking on the issue. I would like to analyze the difficulties inherent in the use of these words and in the assumptions behind them. I will be making a number of historical references in doing so, but it is not my intent to present anything like a history. The history of American education is told elsewhere, and the important transition in the 1840s to which I have alluded has already been analyzed in depth.[5] For my purposes here I need only

---

5. For primary citations of articles and books, see the discussion, refer-

outline the main elements of the public philosophy that emerged in the early 1800s as the basis for a new experiment in American public education—a public philosophy shared by Thomas Jefferson, Noah Webster, Benjamin Rush, and Horace Mann among others that has structured the language of the Supreme Court justices quoted above.[6]

Jefferson, Webster, Rush, Mann, and other early national leaders like them were convinced of the importance of families, churches, and schools. In fact, they recognized that the new republic was fashioned by a common morality that these institutions had promoted and nurtured. But they still worried about the long-term future of the republic. Jefferson, among others, had insisted on the disestablishment of the church—something that was built into the federal Constitution but that had not been carried through in all the states by the early 1800s.[7] With a growing diversity of states, families, churches, and schools in the future, how could the new country hang together over the long run without some means of inculcating and promoting common republican virtues?

The answer to which many of these early leaders were drawn was the idea of the common public school. The particular aspect of this answer that concerns us here is their conception of schooling as an extension of government's responsibility to promote common citizenship and common republican values. Supporting the idea of the common school was the unquestioned assumption that government has an original prerogative to build and administer schools as part of its very nature—as an expression of its responsibility to protect and nurture citizens. This assumption grows from Greek and Roman conceptions of the polis and the republic. The institutions of church and family were ignored or deprecated when it came to a consideration of common citizenship training. The diverse schools that already existed in the early 1800s were also taken lightly or scorned by those who wanted common schools. Jefferson and others did not believe that the new republic could depend on private, independent, diversified efforts at moral and civic training. These theorists never seriously considered the possibility that government could promote its educational concerns by supporting the

---

ences, and notes in Rockne McCarthy, James Skillen, and William Harper, *Disestablishment a Second Time: Genuine Pluralism for American Schools* (Grand Rapids: Eerdmans, 1982), pp. 52-72, 146-53.

6. This discussion depends on a more elaborate but differently focused treatment in *Disestablishment a Second Time*, pp. 15-51.

7. See Carl H. Esbeck, "Religion and a Neutral State: Imperative or Impossibility," *Cumberland Law Review*, 15 (1984-85): 74-75; and McCarthy et al., *Disestablishment a Second Time*, pp. 4-14.

diversity of schools already in existence and by protecting the freedom of parents to choose from among those schools for their children's education. The ancient republican philosophy, revived by "enlightened" leaders, was simply adopted as the truth, on the basis of which common public schools would be organized for the sake of public well-being. Education became a department of state.

What was this philosophy of life, government, and schooling that captured the hearts and minds of these early leaders? How could they have had such a strong sense of civic virtue and republican government but so little regard for the independent role of families, schools, and churches in society?

The philosophy in question is predicated on the interrelation of two "centers of gravity," so to speak. The first center is the individual person; the second is the universal law of nature embracing both physical necessity and moral rights. The philosophy holds that these two poles are intimately dependent on one another, but at the same time it defines them somewhat in opposition to one another.[8] It suggests, for example, that the *individual* possesses rights and an identity in relation to the *universal* law of nature and that the universal law of nature defines and supports free, sovereign individuals. Human beings are *social* creatures, it says, and yet any organization or association is built by free individuals coming together as independent persons without prior social constraint.

For Jefferson and many others in his day, this individualistic/universalistic view of human nature entailed no detailed social or political philosophy. In other words, it did not imply a recognition that different social institutions had to be interpreted and explained differently. Jefferson did not even have a developed theory of the state as one particular institution among others. He wrote much about how a government could be established by autonomous individuals and about how it should be limited with respect to those free individuals, but he wrote little or nothing about the distinct nature of the political community in contrast to families, schools, churches, and the like. Essentially he viewed every social institution as a voluntary society. As Daniel Boorstin describes it,

> The Jeffersonian natural "rights" philosophy was thus a declaration of inability or unwillingness to give positive form to the concept of community, or to face the need for defining explicitly

---

8. See McCarthy et al., *Disestablishment a Second Time*, pp. 30-37; see also Hafen, "The Constitutional Status of Marriage . . . ," pp. 470, 570.

the moral ends to be served by government. From the point of view of the individual, "rights" have a positive enough look: they validate his power under certain circumstances and in certain ways to express his individuality without hindrance. But from the point of view of the community, "rights" have a negative implication: they prescribe what the community *cannot* do. They warn where government dare not go, without suggesting where it ought to go.[9]

Not only did this philosophy lack a sufficiently positive content for its idea of political community, but it said even less about the distinct nature and purpose of the family, the school, the church, the economic enterprise, and so forth. The "natural rights" philosophy conceived of human beings in the Stoic fashion—as a species of rational individuals who are free to create institutions, including a universal voluntary association (a republic), with a set of common moral principles that accord with the rationality of universal natural law. By definition, these individuals and their associations, guided by natural reason, would not confront problems of mixed or conflicting allegiances to home, school, church, state, and trade. All diversity is explained or resolved by reference to the universal moral law and the free individual.

The individual, from this point of view, is independent and free, yet at the same time bound by the universal moral law. On the one hand, the individual is free and autonomous, subject to no one; on the other hand, every individual is subject to the same universal moral order that excludes the problem of difference among any of them. At some points in Jefferson's writings one finds him emphasizing the priority and supremacy of the free individual. At other points he stresses the superiority of the republic as the highest embodiment of the universal moral identity of humanity.

For Jefferson and other "enlightened" thinkers of his day, the individual's freedom and potential for self-realization require the adoption of a natural rights philosophy that can liberate one from the shackles of religious myth, biased opinion, and subjection to parochial interests of church and family. The highest moral and social purpose of human beings, they believed, is to be found in the building of a republic that embodies the natural moral order of the universe.

To understand the inner tension between the "individual" and the "universal" in Jefferson's thought, consider Jefferson's interpreta-

---

9. Boorstin, *The Lost World of Thomas Jefferson* (Boston: Beacon Press, 1966), p. 195.

tion of how authority functions in a republic. The first moral principle of a republic, Jefferson argued, is that the will of the majority "is the fundamental law of every society of individuals of equal rights." The majority expresses the will of society even if that majority is decided by just a single vote. The only alternative to majority rule, Jefferson thought, is the use of force, which inevitably ends in military despotism. Majority rule is the natural right of a group or "collection" of people, just as self-determination is the natural right of every individual. "Every man and every body of men on earth," said Jefferson, "possess the right of self-government. They receive it with their being from the hand of nature. Individuals exercise it by their single will; collections of men by that of their majority; for the law of the *majority* is the natural law for every society of men."[10]

Within the public realm of a healthy republic, therefore, Jefferson did not envision unresolvable conflict growing from diverse social allegiances. A single will of the majority would direct the society as if it were a one-willed body. The rights of individuals would be protected as part of the very definition of a just republic that represents universal law, but in the public arena the minority would willingly submit to the will of the majority as if to their very own public will.

It is perhaps easy now to see how the early republican view of education arose. On the one hand, the human race is made up of individuals, each of whom needs to learn how to live independently. On the other hand, the republic must hold together with a common will built on the universal moral consensus that is written into the natural law. Education is simply the process by which individuals are brought to maturity—both to their own autonomous independence and to a common sharing in the universal rational consensus of society. Schools, families, churches, and other institutions are not equal and diverse partners in a complex society, distinguishable from the government of the republic and deserving public recognition in society. No, they are voluntary associations built by individuals and therefore subject to majority will in the republic and to the individual's autonomy in private life. Education (and therefore the system of schools that would offer the proper education) is simply an extension of government.

Jefferson did not think he was discriminating against families, schools, and churches in his bid for common public schools. He simply

---

10. Jefferson, quoted by Robert Healey in *Jefferson on Religion and Education* (New Haven: Yale University Press, 1962), p. 43; see also *Writings of Thomas Jefferson*, 10 vols., ed. Paul L. Ford (New York: Knickerbocker Press, 1892-99), 5: 205-6.

assumed that the moral training conducted in homes, churches, and most schools was, by definition, *private* education and thereby insufficient as a basis for the common republic, the *public* order.

Jefferson, Rush, Webster, and Mann assumed that *principalship* in education belongs to government and that it ought to be exercised by establishing public *agencies* for common education—namely, the common schools. By the very nature of this outlook on life, parental responsibility in education would have to take second place, and the role of churches and other schools would have to accommodate themselves to the central and prior responsibility of public government for the common good.

Writing to John Adams in 1813, Jefferson explained that his plan for education in Virginia was part of a larger program to replace an "artificial aristocracy" (including the clergy) with a natural aristocracy, and to do this by nurturing "equality of condition" among the people, raising them to the level at which they would be able by their own power and good judgment "to select the able and good for the direction of government."[11] Jefferson viewed the clergy as tyrants enslaving the minds of the people, just as he viewed kings and wealthy artistocrats as tyrants enslaving people's bodies and properties. He wanted to overthrow all tyrants, including the clergy and other aristocrats, and elevate the people to autonomous freedom. And he sought to do it by means of a uniform, common public education for every citizen.

Notice the tension, however, between individual freedom and common public molding of all individuals. It is this tension that Justice Douglas was referring to when he said that while the evolution of the public school system was admirable for "those who think like Madison and Jefferson, it had disadvantages. The main one is that a state system may attempt to mold all students alike according to views of the dominant group and to discourage the emergence of individual idiosyncrasies." Jefferson equated the individually free American with the "perfectly homogeneous" American. He believed that each person should be "free" to sit at the feet of a government-appointed educational aristocrat to learn how to be a free citizen.

The structural framework of this enlightened, republican philosophy is not necessarily connected with the sacred/secular distinction. In fact, Jefferson acknowledged that the common schools would definitely

---

11. See *The Life and Selected Writings of Thomas Jefferson*, ed. Adrienne Koch and William Peden (New York: Modern Library, 1944), pp. 632-34.

be inculcating religious and moral values, that they would not be "neutral" or "secularistic" in our contemporary sense. Rather, Jefferson and the others made an important distinction between the common public order under government and the private realm of belief and conviction outside of government. Education worthy of and necessary for a vital republic belongs in the common public realm, they maintained, and cannot be left to private institutions.

What Jefferson wanted to elevate in public was the nonsectarian, the truly universal—as opposed to the sectarian and the merely parochial, which he wanted to keep in private. Of course, these distinctions make full and agreeable sense only to those with the same mindset as Jefferson. And this unveils the true dogmatism and biased sectarian character of that philosophy. Although Jefferson and others believed that the true republican faith was common and universal, their conviction was, after all, but one faith among many both in their day and in ours. Jefferson's plan, if successful, would be nothing less than the establishment of one dominant faith and moral system to the exclusion of all others in the public arena.[12]

Jefferson was not entirely unconscious of his bias. In private letters he confessed his hope that the changes brought about by a common public school system would include "a quiet euthanasia of the heresies of bigotry and fanaticism which have so long triumphed over human reason."[13] Jefferson's plan would not really exclude dogmas from the public schools; it would merely substitute the dogma of rationalistic empiricism and enlightened moralism for those dogmas guiding most of the families, schools, and churches of his time.

It is not my purpose here to debate the extent of Jefferson's dogmatism, however. I simply want to make the point that the philosophy that guided him to his political and educational conclusions led directly to a plan for public schools that would mold all citizens into a common republican faith. And that faith, he believed, would enable them to ex-

---

12. For more on this point, see David Little's excellent studies "The Origins of Perplexity: Civil Religion and Moral Belief in the Thought of Thomas Jefferson," in *American Civil Religion*, ed. Russell E. Richey and Donald G. Jones (New York: Harper & Row, 1974), pp. 185-210; and "Thomas Jefferson's Religious Views and Their Influence on the Supreme Court's Interpretation of the First Amendment," *Catholic University Law Review* 26 (Fall 1976): 57-72.

13. Jefferson, in a letter to William Short dated 31 October 1819, in Koch and Peden, *Life and Writings*, p. 694.

press and accede to the will of the majority in public life. Diverse opinions and sectarian convictions should be kept in private.

Not until after the 1840s, following school battles in Boston and New York, was a firm connection finally made between the sacred/secular distinction and the private/public distinction. New York and Boston were receiving large numbers of Roman Catholic immigrants, and some believed this influx to constitute a threat to the common public order. The Catholics began to appeal for the same support of their schools that the Protestants received for theirs. In order to sustain privileged funding for their schools to the exclusion of Catholic schools, the dominant Protestant majorities reacted to the pluralizing threat by labeling their schools (which were not yet integrated into anything like a modern public school system) "nonsectarian" and labeling the religious schools of the Catholics "sectarian."[14]

The designation of "secular" or "nonreligious" was not yet applied to the schools of the majority during the 1840s, but the majority's successful efforts against the Catholics did lead to the institutionalization of a system of government-established, government-run schools acceptable to the majority and distinguishable from what they called the "sectarian" schools. The public legal consequence was the development of a formal distinction between common public schools and private sectarian schools. Although both sets of schools served the public purpose of training citizens and both were very religious, the one system nevertheless became identified with the public order within the framework of Jefferson's republican philosophy. The other system was relegated to the arena of private choice and subjected to what the majority believed was a legitimate discrimination.

As American society became both more diversified and, to a certain extent, more secularized during the next 130 years, the common public schools were forced to keep pace with legitimate public demands for nondiscrimination. Given the framework established in the 1840s, there seemed to be no alternatives to the gradual elimination of features and functions that did not accord with majority will or with general civil rights laws. Eventually, for example, Bible readings and prayers were removed from the public schools. Discrimination against nongovernment schools was formalized and solidified. The public schools became ever more fully identified with what is "public," "secu-

---

14. For more on the situation in the 1840s in New York and Boston, see McCarthy et al., *Disestablishment a Second Time*, pp. 52-72. For information on the New York situation only, see Ravitch, *The Great School Wars*, pp. 3-76.

lar," and "nonreligious," while nonpublic schools, most of which had a religious identity or affiliation, were identified with private choice and opting out. By the time the U.S. Supreme Court began to hear school cases, the ruling republican philosophy of Jefferson and others (further shaped by the religious/secular distinction) was axiomatic.

With only a few exceptions, the U.S. Supreme Court did not begin to hear school cases before the 1940s. One of the exceptions (which was very significant but could have been a good deal more significant) was the 1925 case of *Pierce v. Society of Sisters* 268 U.S. 510 (1925). In this case the Supreme Court upheld the right of parents to choose schools for their children other than those established by the state of Oregon, a right that had been denied by an Oregon law.[15]

The Supreme Court's decision would seem to reflect the tradition that recognizes parental principalship in education. It seems to contradict the contention that a public school monopoly founded on a Jeffersonian philosophy has come to dominate American schooling since the 1840s. The decision in the *Pierce* case would seem to suggest that parents do have a fundamental and prior right to choose the agency for educating their children. The decision appears to call into question the state's preeminent right to appoint the agencies for the education of its citizens and cedes primary choice to the parents. And if parents may legitimately choose either state agencies or nonstate agencies for the education of their children, then should not the government act without discrimination in regard to those parental choices? Should not the agencies (the schools) selected by parents be treated so that each can enjoy the same public recognition and funding?

Here is where the contradictions and inequities become quite clear. As a matter of fact, the Supreme Court did not overturn state primacy in education in the *Pierce* case. It did no more than guarantee the right of parents to opt out of the preeminent public school system if conscience required it and if they could afford it. Parental *principalship* was not fully acknowledged. Oregon was allowed to continue the practice of channeling all public funds and public recognition to its own agencies while merely tolerating the private right of parents to opt out at their own expense.

Beginning in the 1940s with major decisions such as *Everson v. Board of Education of Ewing Township* (330 U.S. 1 [1947]) and

---

15. For more on this, see especially Stephen Arons, "The Separation of School and State: *Pierce* Reconsidered," *Harvard Educational Review*, 46 (1976): 76 ff.

McCollum v. Board of Education (333 U.S. 203 [1948]), the Supreme Court sought ways to handle particular problems within the context of essentially Jeffersonian philosophy and assumptions. To date, one can hardly find a reference in the Court's rulings to parental rights and responsibilities in education except within contexts that presume governmental principalship entailing constant favoritism toward its own schools. And this is almost always framed in terms of the religious/secular dichotomy.

The so-called three-part test that the Supreme Court now uses in school decisions involving religion is a test for government's dealing with Establishment Clause cases generally:

> First, the statute [a state or federal law] must have a secular legislative purpose; second, its principal or primary effect must be one that neither advances nor inhibits religion . . . ; finally the statute must not foster "an excessive government entanglement with religion." (Burger, *Lemon* I, 403 U.S. 602 [1971], pp. 612-13)

This is the test Chief Justice Burger believes can justify state aid to "church-related" schools by means of "secular, neutral, or nonideological services, facilities, or materials."

This argument, which treats books, lunches, health services, and buses as if they are not an integral part of a school's identity and purpose, can be understood only in terms of the chief justice's prior commitment to the religious/secular dichotomy and to its assumed connection with the distinction between public and private schools. But this commitment makes it impossible for Burger to recognize the identity of a school apart from the categories of state and church. He insists on dividing the world into sacred and secular realms, equating the former exclusively with the church and the latter exclusively with the state, and he is thus unable to take into account the real identities and functions of families and schools. Instead of trying to overcome the confusion in the Court's determination of what is "sacred" and what is "secular," he simply appeals to the public to rekindle the old Jeffersonian faith that sustains those unquestioned but very problematic assumptions.

In an earlier decision, *Abington School District v. Schempp* (374 U.S. 203 [1963]), the Court ruled against a Pennsylvania law that had required Bible reading in the public school, ruling that it violated the Establishment Clause of the First Amendment. Notice the language of Justice Clark, who wrote the majority opinion:

> The place of religion in our society is an exalted one, achieved

through a long tradition of reliance on the home, the church, and the inviolable citadel of the individual heart and mind. We have come to recognize through bitter experience that *it is not within the power of government to invade that citadel, whether its purpose or effect be to aid or oppose, to advance or retard. In the relationship between man and religion, the state is firmly committed to a position of neutrality.* (P. 226)

This statement gives evidence of all the problematic implications of the Court's ambivalent position. Clark assumes that religion is unambiguously private, having its identity entirely outside the state. Partly because of this unproven and unquestioned assumption, he overlooks one of the central institutions in our society that has promulgated our exalted religious traditions—namely, the schools. He refers to the home, church, and individual heart as the great centers of religion. This is a central dogma in the ideology we have been discussing, but it distorts and hides the simple fact that schools were the centers of Christian training for decades into the nineteenth century, and even by the end of last century, Protestantism, in both its pietistic and its republican religiosity, thoroughly penetrated the so-called nonsectarian, public schools.

Clark also assumes that the government can in fact be neutral toward the citadel of the human heart and mind while it controls and finances the public school system. But the establishment of one monopolistic public school system, controlled by local and state political institutions, is not and never has been a neutral secular establishment. It was not neutral as Jefferson and others conceived it; it was not neutral when it was controlled by the Protestants; it was not neutral when the Bible *was* required for devotional reading; and it is not neutral now that individual children are "protected" from hearing the Bible read. The question is not whether neutrality can be maintained by permitting or banning Bible reading in public schools but whether a single, favored, public school system can guarantee neutrality.

It is certainly proper for the government to prevent discrimination and ensure evenhanded treatment of all citizens. We should be neither surprised by nor critical of government's efforts to end racial discrimination, religious discrimination, or any other kind of unfairness. But to be truly fair and nondiscriminatory, government must deal with all of reality. Governments and the Supreme Court have not yet accounted for the real identities of schools and families. These institutions have identities that cannot be treated fairly in public law simply on the basis of universal governmental regulations respecting the civil rights of individual citizens. Government has no right, constitutional or otherwise, to predefine any of these institutions as either exclusively religious or exclusively secular, for example. It has no right to define the family or the school as a department of state. It has no right to ignore the original rights and identities of families and schools (not to mention churches) as it goes about educating citizens.[16]

There is no just way to respect the educational process and the rights of families without treating the true diversity of schools and families in a nondiscriminatory and equitable fashion. The effort to make education a single, exclusive, homogeneous process delivering services directly to citizens from the government will inevitably distort the very nature of education in the eyes of many citizens. Children are not merely individuals in a republic. They are children in homes, members of churches, students at different schools, and so on. Many citizens reject the fundamental assumptions of Jefferson's public philosophy. They would argue that, at least in some cases, schools can be treated justly only if, like families, churches, and business enterprises, they are not made into departments of state. To ignore the diverse opinions and convictions of even a minority of families and teachers in the United States is to ignore the demands of justice for a nondiscriminatory treatment of all citizens.

Even in the case of *Wisconsin v. Yoder* (406 U.S. 205 [1972]), in which the Supreme Court granted a partial immunity from compulsory school attendance to an Amish group in Wisconsin, the majority opinion followed the well-established lines of the prevailing mindset. Chief Justice Burger stated that the Court's evaluation of the Amish claims had to determine whether "their religious faith and their mode of life are, as they claim, inseparable and interdependent." Said Burger, "A way of life, however virtuous and admirable, may not be interposed as a barrier to reasonable state regulation of education if it is based on purely secular considerations; to have the protection of the Religion Clauses, the claims must be rooted in religious belief" (p. 215).

Burger assumes that religion is so distinguishable from the rest of life that it is possible to differentiate a life (or part of a life) guided by religion from a life (or part of a life) guided by purely "secular considerations." He also assumes that the First Amendment defines religion in a way that is sufficient to keep it from being misused by irreligious or nonreligious persons. And the Chief Justice is convinced,

---

16. On this, see Tyll van Geel, "The Search for Constitutional Limits on Governmental Authority to Inculcate Youth," *Texas Law Review*, October 1983, pp. 199-297, especially pp. 201-2.

finally, that if the religion clauses cannot be appealed to, then "secular" people with "secular" claims have no grounds for escaping the majoritarian educational requirements that are imposed on all citizens no matter how virtuous and admirable may be the education they might prefer to give their children.

The Jeffersonian rationalism of the Chief Justice could not be expressed more clearly than in these words from his *Yoder* decision. The very concept of ordered liberty, he says,

> precludes allowing every person to make his own standards on matters of conduct in which society as a whole has important interests. Thus, if the Amish asserted their claims because of their subjective evaluation and rejection of the contemporary secular values accepted by the majority, much as Thoreau rejected the social values of his time and isolated himself at Walden Pond, their claims would not rest on a religious basis. Thoreau's choice was philosophical and personal rather than religious, and such belief does not rise to the demands of the Religion Clauses. (Pp. 215-16)

Clearly, Burger believes that the "secular values of the majority" ought to have moral authority over "society as a whole." No adequate account is given of families and schools and churches in this judgment. The justices are prepared to allow people to find relief from (and a chance to opt out of) the requirement of majoritarian control within the public domain only if they can appeal to the religion clauses of the First Amendment in a way that the justices accept. Burger's entire argument presupposes the religious/secular qualification of the distinction between "private diversity" and "public unity."

Justice Burger has not demonstrated why the Amish way of life is religious while his own Jeffersonian rationalism is not religious. Nor has he explained his grounds for assuming that Thoreau's deep convictions were nonreligious; in fact Thoreau's personal and quite integral life was pointedly religious. Nor has he explained why he contrasts an Amish *community* with an *individual* (Thoreau); they represent two patently different kinds of human realities. The argument is simply a continuation of the one made by Protestants in the nineteenth century to distinguish the legitimate public consensus from the parochial wishes of minorities. The latter may be allowed to opt out of the majority's public world if the minority is religious and private enough and willing to "do their thing" without public expense.

At first glance, the Supreme Court's decision in *Mueller v. Allen* (103 S.Ct. 3062 [1983]) suggests that a major change might be taking place both in Minnesota and at the highest U.S. judicial level. In the *Mueller* case, the Court upheld a Minnesota law granting state income tax deductions for costs incurred by parents in the education of their children at elementary and secondary schools without regard to whether those schools are private or public. The majority opinion, written by Justice Rehnquist, indicates approval of the "secular" purpose of the Minnesota law, since it does not target private schools exclusively but supports any educational expense. Moreover, since the aid comes by way of a tax calculation by the parent at home, the law can hardly be accused of fostering excessive government entanglement in religion.

The fact that the Court supported the Minnesota law is indeed significant, since it shows respect for a state's effort to distribute financial aid more equitably to all parents, thereby showing sensitivity to parental choice in the education of children. Nevertheless, *Mueller v. Allen* should not be received too optimistically. The language and reasoning of the Court have not changed significantly, and the criteria remain the same. The Court has simply allowed a new mechanism whereby Minnesota can aid parents who are "opting out" of the public system to use "private" schools. The framework of thought about what is "private," "public," "sacred," and "secular" remains the same.[17]

The fact that the Court has not radically altered its assumptions was demonstrated most recently in 1985 in two more school cases. On 1 July, the Court ruled 5-4 against the cities of Grand Rapids and New York in *School District of the City of Grand Rapids et al. v. Ball et al.* and *Aguilar et al. v. Felton et al.* Through somewhat different programs, the two cities were providing special educational services to nonpublic school students.

In Grand Rapids the city was offering both "shared time" and "community education" programs in nonpublic schools to nonpublic students at public expense. These either supplemented the core curriculum of those schools during regular school hours or added voluntary offerings for students after the regular school day. In New York the city was using federal funds under Title I to pay salaries of public school employees to teach special courses to educationally deprived children from low-income families in nonpublic schools.

In both cases the Court ruled the programs unconstitutional because they "entangled" the government too much in "religion" and

---

17. For several appreciative evaluations of the *Mueller* case, see the entire issue of *Educational Freedom* 16 (Spring-Summer 1983). Note also the amicus curiae brief filed before the Supreme Court on that case by Edward M. Gaffney, Jr.

therefore violated the Establishment Clause. The language used and the arguments made are still essentially the same.

Within the framework of those faulty assumptions, however, the dissenting justices are becoming ever sharper in spotting the inconsistencies and contradictions in the arguments. Justice Rehnquist dissented from the majority, pointing out the "Catch-22 paradox" that the Court has created for itself. The Court expects state and local governments to supervise the services they provide, to make sure that religion is not established by government. But then, in these cases, the Court ruled that the close supervision provided by the government amounted to an illegitimate entanglement of government in religious institutions.

Justice O'Connor also criticized the majority opinion, pointing to the fact that in nineteen years of New York's special services to needy nonpublic school students "there has never been a single incident in which an . . . instructor 'subtly or overtly' attempted to 'indoctrinate the students in particular religious tenets at public expense.'" The irony of these decisions, as Justice O'Connor indicated, is that if these same educational services had been offered in a setting off the property of the private schools, the Court probably would have accepted them as it did similar programs in its decision in the 1977 *Wolman v. Walter* case.

We are left, then, to wonder if the Court will ever move to a new framework for judging these cases. Is there a way to overcome the predicament in which the Court and the American people find themselves?

THE FUTURE OF AMERICAN SCHOOLING: WHAT MUST BE CHANGED?

Having pursued my analysis this far, I believe it is now possible to show what must change if we are to extricate ourselves from the false dilemmas and unresolvable contradictions over education policy and law in the United States today. Some of the chief ingredients of cultural and educational reality have been overlooked, excluded, or misidentified from the early 1800s to the present. The ruling assumptions about governmental primacy and sacred/secular stratification are self-contradictory and self-defeating in the realm of education. Only by returning to examine what was left out and what was distorted in this historical process (as it was guided by mistaken assumptions) can we understand the reason for the contemporary problems and pose a new alternative.

Return for a moment to the *Pierce v. Society of Sisters* case in 1925. The Supreme Court upheld the right of parents to choose schools for their children other than those established by the state of Oregon, but it did not really overthrow the preeminence of state principalship in education. At best, then, the decision recognized that parental authority in education cannot be discarded altogether. At worst, it seemed to seal forever the second-class and subordinate status of parents in the realm of education.

This act of discrimination against parents (and against any nongovernment agency that parents choose) is usually justified by the argument that the parents' choice of a nongovernment school is a private, usually religious choice that cannot be supported by equitable public recognition and funding without entangling government in the establishment of religion. But notice what is overlooked and distorted by this Jeffersonian, Enlightenment bias. Families and schools are not treated in their own right. Simply ask yourself: Are families and schools religious or secular institutions? If a school truly educates students to become mature, competent, and employable adults and respectful citizens, is it private or public? What if a parent chooses to send his or her child to a nongovernment school that makes no religious claim? Obviously, in that case, the religious/secular distinction does not apply. Why, in that case, should government withhold equitable funding and recognition from that school and from those parents? If the answer is that government has the primacy in selecting schools for its citizens, then it is obviously relegating parental choice to second place even without appeal to the religious/secular distinction. This is certainly in conformity with Jefferson's philosophy, but it is plainly discriminatory unless it is the case that all educational responsibility resides with the government without exception. But if that is so, the Court's ruling in the case of *Pierce v. Society of Sisters* cannot be legitimate; the government would then be obligated to overturn the *Pierce* decision and make it clear that parents have no right to select the education of their children. If the *Pierce* decision is to be maintained, the inner conflict between parental principalship and government principalship will have to be resolved in a manner that brings equity and fairness.

The *Mueller v. Allen* case shows that the Supreme Court and the state of Minnesota (at least) are *not* trying to push in the direction of consistent public exclusivism with regard to educational principalship. The Court supported Minnesota's small effort to provide some tax relief to parents sending their children to nonpublic schools. However, the basic legal rationale for this state law and for the Court's decision has not changed. Government still assumes the first right of principalship in education and directs educational moneys to its public schools alone.

Those who choose nonstate schools are still viewed as "opting out" of the public system. And even though parents choosing nonpublic schools now get a little personal tax relief in Minnesota, it is a minor and inequitable "break" compared with the benefits gained by parents sending their children to public schools.

By monopolizing public recognition and funds for its own schools, government denies equity to teachers, parents, families, and nongovernment schools. It thereby fails in its obligation to treat citizens with fairness. A little financial relief for "private" school parents helps, but it serves more to underscore than to resolve the continuing inequity of the private/public dualism.

Regarding the religious/secular distinction, we might well ask on what grounds the government assumes a right to grant itself a monopoly over the "secular." May the government claim sovereignty over everything secular, without limits? And on what grounds does government have the right to decide that "religion" belongs primarily if not only to churches or to church-related institutions?[18] If parents choose, on self-confessed religious grounds, to educate their children in a school that is established by an organization other than a church for the purpose of giving a thorough education to students in the light of religious principles, does that create a "religious" problem for the courts? It does if "religion" is identified exclusively with churches, because there would be no church connection in such a case. If some parents choose not to send their children to a public school because they do not like its philosophy of education, is that a religious choice or a secular choice? What if they choose to teach them at home?

The point of these questions is to show that the use of the First Amendment in school issues is frequently misleading. The First Amendment does not mention families and schools. In fact, it does not even refer to churches. The Amendment is usually interpreted, however, in such a way that religion is identified with churches and private conscience and government is assumed to enjoy a monopoly over what is secular. Families and schools are not treated by the courts as having identities independent of church or state, of the "religious" or the "secular." But family life and education and business can be as "secular" as politics: the government has no right to claim a monopoly over the "sec-

---

18. George C. Freeman III analyzes several important issues of this sort in "The Misguided Search for the Constitutional Definition of 'Religion,'" *Georgetown Law Journal* 71 (1983): 1519-65.

ular." Likewise, families, schools, and businesses can be as religious as the churches: churches do not monopolize religion.

So, whether or not "religion" is involved in education, the real question concerns the nature of, and the proper responsibility for, education. We are brought back to the first and most important question of who has what kind of responsibility for education.

We can resolve problems stemming from the false sacred/secular dichotomy, I think, by changing our assumptions about *principalship* and *agency* in education. But we cannot take this step without giving serious attention to the importance of government's responsibility for justice and equity in society. The ongoing ambiguity and contradiction in American education policy will never be satisfactorily resolved until we recognize both that government has a legitimate and proper concern for the well-being of citizens—including their educational well-being—and also that government cannot do justice to everyone involved in education until it recognizes that parents hold the full obligation of principalship for their children. To change assumptions at this point leads, necessarily, to changes in assumptions about the meaning of public/private and sacred/secular distinctions.

Let us begin with the family. As long as children are minors, parents should be held accountable for their children's well-being. This is not to say that parents have to do everything for their children and that government may do nothing. To the contrary, children are also citizens with basic rights that need to be protected by government. But the rights and responsibilities of parents to care for their children should not be taken away by a governmental mandate that destroys their responsibility as *principals* in the education of their children.

True parental principalship cannot be acknowledged, however, without rejecting once and for all the claims of principalship by government. Even where government fulfills principal responsibilities for some of its minor citizens (orphans, for example), it should do so in loco parentis, not as if it holds original principalship.

In advocating this fundamental change in assumptions—rejecting government's principalship and acknowledging only parental principalship for the education of minors—I am not, however, advocating the complete privatization of education. Only the false dichotomy inherent in an individualist/universalist philosophy leads in this direction. To the contrary, I would insist on the necessity of recognizing the rights and identity of the family as family—something that is neither an individual person nor a mere department of state. Government should neither swallow up family members by treating them simply as citizens, thus abrogating their rights and identities as family members, nor accept the total isolation and autonomy of those persons as if their individuality gives them some right to absolute privacy and freedom from public accountability. The proper response is for government to acknowledge the family, with its inherent parental responsibility for the care and education of minor children, and at the same time accept its own responsibility for the public protection of all its citizens, most of whom also happen to be members of families.[19] I will have more to say about the government's responsibility later.

Second, we must change the focus of our attention, if not our fundamental assumptions, about the nature of educational agencies—the schools. Throughout our entire history we have had many kinds of schools. At no time has the government's system of public schools entailed the exclusion of all other schools, nor has this public school system ever educated all children. Before the 1840s most schools were independent of direct government management. Even after the 1840s a significant percentage (five to twenty percent) of American schools were nongovernment schools. This fact alone bears testimony to the reality that educational agencies need not be government-owned and -operated in order to function as agencies of education. It also tells us that the school is not simply an extension of the government's standard bureaucracy for enforcing rules and providing general services. Even government schools usually possess a sufficient autonomy, ranging from independent budgets to separate elections for school board members, to indicate that the "public" character of those schools does not mean that the educational process within them has been absorbed into general governmental lawmaking.

This means that we have to give special attention to the nature of a school. A school is an agency for education. It is built on a philosophy of education; it hires teachers who have different ideas about how to train students in different disciplines; it must stand in loco parentis and thereby deal amicably and in a trustworthy fashion with parents; it takes in *students*, who then take on a role that can be distinguished from that of *child* in a family and *citizen* in the civil community. In other words, schools are schools and not simply extensions of families or the government. They have a life of their own with an identity and quality peculiar to them. Government must acknowledge the full reality of schools just

---

19. On rights of families and other institutions and association, see Rockne McCarthy et al., *Society, State, and Schools* (Grand Rapids: Eerdmans, 1981), pp. 63-78; and Hafen, "Constitutional Status of Marriage. . . ."

as it does the reality of families. Government does not deal with individual citizens-in-general; it deals with citizens who are at the same time family members and school participants, among many other things.

The rightful recognition of schools as schools would not entail the government's relinquishing all concern for education. It does not even imply that the government should close down all of its own "agencies" of education. It rather calls on government to look on schools, including its own, as distinct agencies of education instead of mere departments of state. In concert with other changes I am suggesting here, this change in perspective would make all the difference in the world.

Government *does* have a responsibility to secure public justice for all its citizens. Among other things, this means recognizing the rights and responsibilities of various institutions and associations that are *not* departments of state—such as families, churches, schools, business enterprises, and the like. Indeed, it is government's responsibility to see that individual citizens, families, schools, and so on are not unjustly discriminated against. The Greek Orthodox Church should enjoy the same public rights and protection as the Presbyterians and the Baptists and members of all churches. A black child should have the same rights and privileges as a white or Oriental child.

When it comes to education, a government might well decide (as our states have done) that fairness, equity, and equal opportunity for its citizens require that each child should benefit from a certain amount of education, or at least that each should reach certain proficiency standards by certain ages in life. The debate about the details of this type of public concern and responsibility can go in a number of directions and embrace a host of legitimate "public health and welfare" concerns. Many questions must be answered: Should schooling be required up to a certain age or should the government merely require the passing of certain tests? Should every child be required to learn English, to master some American and Western history, to participate in driver's education? The questions can go on and on. Though they might not be easily resolved, might never meet with universal public consensus, they are legitimate questions for governments (state, local, and federal) to be asking and resolving for the sake of the equitable well-being of all citizens.

Nevertheless, all these questions should, in the future, be asked at the governmental level (legislative, judicial, and executive) within a framework that takes for granted both the principalship of parents in the education of their children and the right of schools to be schools in offering their services for the education of these children. How, in this case, will public law have to change?

The first major consequence of this shift in assumptions will be to open up genuine parental choice of schooling for children.[20] The present form of choice that parents have is either to use the district public school or to opt out of that system at their own expense. This simply is not a choice for many with low incomes, and it is an unfair choice even for those with sufficient income. If parents are truly the principals in the education of their children, then the only way government can do justice to them is to recognize their principalship. No matter how much good the government wants to do for its citizens through education, if it tries to perform that service while denying parental rights, it will end up doing injustice. By analogy, no matter how much good a government may want to do for the religious well-being of its citizens, if it tries to offer religious services that deny the rights of churches to be churches, it will do injustice and thereby do what is bad, not what is good. How, then, can parental choice be respected properly and equitably?

The only way that genuine parental choice among different educational agencies can be realized is to prevent public law from giving unjust privilege to its own public school agencies. In other words, in addition to recognizing parents as the principals in the education of their children, we must recognize the agencies these parents choose. Every school must have the same legal and financial opportunity to open its doors to the public to offer its services. Tremendous discrimination now exists because nonpublic schools receive neither public funding nor public recognition (except as private schools).

There are a multitude of things we can do to ensure that a genuine diversity of schools are treated equitably in public law. We need not discuss the many options here. I would simply underscore the point that tax credits or vouchers to help alleviate some of the financial burden for parents who select "private" schools are simply not enough to do full justice in this case. They might offer a first step in the direction of greater equity, but as long as government schools receive privileged

---

20. On this issue generally, see the new journal *Equity and Choice*, published by the Institute of Responsive Education, Boston, Massachusetts. The first issue appeared in fall 1984. See also Joe Nathan, *Free to Teach* (Minneapolis: Winston Press, 1984), especially pp. 141-85. And see the Annual Report on Desegregation in Massachusetts, *Equity, Choice and Effective Urban Education: A Focus on Schools* (April 1985), prepared by Charles L. Glenn, Jr., director of the Bureau of Equal Educational Opportunity of the Massachusetts Department of Education.

treatment as the only legitimate agencies of the ultimate principal in education (the government), public moneys for "private" education will never be distributed in truly proportionate amounts, nor will those expenditures ever be fully legitimate. As things stand, I would have to go along with the contention that public funds cannot legitimately be spent for private purposes. The reason that tax credits or vouchers are even considered today is that most citizens realize there is a public purpose being fulfilled in nongovernment schools. But then the best way to take that into account is to give full recognition to all schools that perform a public service—and that means making all such agencies, both government and nongovernment schools, eligible for parental selection without disqualification or financial inequity.

At this juncture I would like to take up the question of religion. What if some parents select a school that happens to be run by the Roman Catholic Church? If the government supports such a school, whether directly or indirectly, does it become illegitimately entangled in religion or run the danger of establishing a religion? To the contrary, to prohibit parental choice of "religious" schools is to discriminate against some religions as well as against some parents. And an establishment danger would arise only if the government decided to give benefits to those who attend Catholic schools that it does not give to those who attend Presbyterian or public schools. A fair and equitable distribution of funds for the purpose of education as I have been describing it would establish nothing but the value of education in the context of parental choice and freedom for all schools.

I think there is a valid analogy in the chaplaincy program in the armed services. Here the government commissions, pays for, and honors official representatives of various ecclesiastical denominations for their service to those in the armed forces. As long as the government does not give disproportionate benefit to one denomination over another, and as long as members of the services are allowed to make their own religious choices, there is neither undue entanglement nor an establishment.

In the Supreme Court's words, the "secular" (I would rather say "general public") purpose of education legislation should be to promote education for every citizen. If that legislation properly recognizes parental principalship as well as the independence of educational agencies, then its "general public" purpose will be fulfilled if parents can freely choose a legitimate school for their children's education. If the conscience of some parents requires a Catholic parochial school, or a school with a philosophy of education that is Christian or Jewish or

Muslim without being connected with any church, or a school that claims to be nonreligious, then the government would be doing justice both to the parents and to the schools by treating them all equitably with the same degree of public recognition and public funding. Government would be "entangled" in the schools only to the extent that it is responsible for justice in education, not to the extent that it would interfere with parental choices or with the doctrines, philosophies, and curricula of the schools as it now does. No religion would be established; in fact, this is the only way for the government to keep from establishing either religion or irreligion in its own specially privileged agencies. Parents should choose and schools should offer services; the government should not mandate or establish the school agency for education.

This argument requires a change in assumptions about the application of the Establishment Clause of the First Amendment to school cases. It fits well, however, with Carl Esbeck's reformulation of the Court's "three-part" test of secular purpose, neutral primary effect, and nonentanglement. He suggests a formulation that "folds" this three-part test into two elements:

> First, the establishment clause requires that government be neutral toward religion, but not indifferent and never hostile. Second the establishment clause prohibits government action which compromises the independence or integrity of a religious organization, absent some truly exigent threat to public health, safety, peace or order.[21]

Genuine pluralism in education, predicated on parental principalship and equitable treatment of diverse agencies, meets Esbeck's criteria very well insofar as religion is a factor. If the government would call a halt to discrimination with regard to parental choice, it could begin to practice the sort of true neutrality that is neither indifferent nor hostile to the religion or nonreligion of any parent or school. And if it were to recognize schools as schools and families as families, the government could avoid compromising the independence and integrity of any "religious" organization that happens to run a school, whether that organization is an educational association, a church, or whatever. Government could keep its attention focused on the general, educational, public purpose that all schools are supposed to serve.

---

21. Esbeck, "Religion and the Neutral State," p. 86. See also Esbeck's "Establishment Clause Limits on Governmental Interference with Religious Organizations," *Washington and Lee Law Review*, 41 (Spring 1984): 347-420.

In this respect, the entire issue of "religion" versus "secularity" is removed from the arena of education. That was a mistaken connection in the first place. It would never have become an issue had it not been for the way nineteenth-century Protestants tried to remove Catholic schools from public recognition on the grounds of their parochialism and sectarianism. It would never have become an issue if Americans had not misidentified religion with privacy and with churches alone. Religion is not simply what goes on in churches and in some individual consciences; it is also the way many people choose to live, including the way they choose to raise and educate their children. Government has no constitutional right to predefine the limits and scope of religion. Nor does it have the concomitant right to give itself a monopoly over the so-called "secular" world. We have already tried to show that families and schools are important actors in both the so-called "secular" world and the "religious" world. Government must always pay attention to the welfare of the entire public, always mandate (through law) what is in the public interest. If its mandates happen to include providing education for every citizen, then it will have to see to it that the mandate is carried out in a way that does justice to the children, parents, teachers, schools, and other individuals and organizations involved in the process. If some citizens choose to make education part of their religious practice while others prefer to identify schooling with something irreligious or nonreligious, then so be it. That is not government's concern.

Now, finally, let us examine a few of the implications of my proposals for government's responsibility in all this. Is it possible for government to give up claims of principalship in education, recognize with full equity all the agencies that offer educational services, treat education as education rather than as something divided between religious privacy and public secularity, and still ensure that every child will receive the public protection and assistance needed for the sake of the public welfare?

The first thing government will have to do is to make very clear the essentials of public fairness for every citizen—doubtless including such things as "free" education for all, freedom from racial discrimination, freedom from undue hardship for the handicapped and new immigrants, and so on. Many of these characteristics of a just society have not been adequately realized within the present framework of public education. A new pluralistic system could probably do a much better job, although there is of course no way to guarantee that an error-free system could be created. An ongoing commitment will have to be made to do justice to every individual citizen as well as to families and schools and communities. Local, state, and federal governments, along with the courts, will have to keep busy updating laws and changing policies to make sure that education is offered in an equitable manner to every citizen.

Without attempting to prejudge all future government decisions, and without implying that each of the following suggestions is exactly what is needed, I would like to list a few of the things that government might do to fulfill its role in a new pluralistic system.[22]

State governments might, for example, invite any school that wishes to be part of a "public pluralistic system of free schools" to enter the consortium of schools through which each would be given a proportionate amount of public funding (proportionate to the number of students each educates). The terms of entry for a school might include the following (among others):

1. Freedom for each school to define its own philosophy of education.

2. Freedom for each school to hire its teachers in accord with its own philosophy and behavioral standards so long as they meet minimum educational standards for teachers.

3. A requirement that any child who wants to come to that school (whose parents choose it) must be accepted, albeit on the terms of discipline and within the curricular and behavioral standards that the school offers. It does not seem impossible to me that such a requirement could still allow freedom for various specialty schools, such as all-boys or all-girls schools, vocational training schools, college preparatory schools, and so on.

4. The requirement that the school must either participate in an independent accrediting agency (at its own level of schooling) or meet state standards for basic educational competencies, testing, and the like.

5. The requirement that a school may not charge additional tui-

---

22. More elaborate discussions of alternatives for the present and the future are presented in McCarthy et al., *Society, State, and Schools*, pp. 136-44, 170-208; McCarthy et al., *Disestablishment a Second Time*, pp. 107-36; Nathan, *Free to Teach*, pp. 121-40; the entire fall/winter 1984-85 issue of *Educational Freedom* (vol. 18), which is devoted to vouchers; Constance Pepin and David Hunt, "Education Vouchers: Theory and Practice" (a background paper prepared for the Citizens League, Minneapolis, Minnesota, September 1983); Nanette Barrett, *Education Source Book: The State Legislator's Guide for Reform* (Washington: American Legislative Exchange Council, 1985); and Charles L. Glenn, Jr., "Learning from Dutch Education," *The Reformed Journal*, September 1984, pp. 14-17.

tion as a condition for entry beyond the basic per-student amount given by the government. This would not necessarily preclude a school raising additional private funds for its program.

These are simply a few examples. If something like this system were adopted, it would not require the closing or elimination of all nonparticipating schools. There still might be reasons why some schools (or communities such as the Amish) would not want to participate in the public pluralistic system. If they made such a choice, they would of course have to forego the benefits of public support and funding, but that would be their choice rather than government's discriminatory exclusion.

A variation on such a system might entail the government's providing most of the necessary funding through vouchers given directly to parents. In that case, however, government would also have to establish a means by which school buildings and other capital investments would be provided and distributed for use proportionately among all schools.

Details of implementation and ongoing public dispute cannot all be settled here, nor do they have to be. Citizens in some states might, for example, want to debate changing the basis for raising educational moneys from property tax to a state-wide income tax. Transportation, taxation, testing, competency standards—these and many other issues might remain open for public debate.

I will have achieved my purpose here if I do nothing more than to point the way to overcoming the injustices now being suffered by families, schools, and many citizens within the majoritarian system of government-controlled schooling. If the American people can achieve a new consensus that government should promote educational well-being among all its citizens by granting consistent freedom of choice to parents and an equitable freedom of opportunity to all schools, then the other details can be worked out case by case, year to year.

A Study of Religion and Traditional Values in Public School Textbooks

Paul C. Vitz

The general purpose of this project was to investigate systematically how religion and traditional values are represented in today's public school textbooks. The general finding is that public school textbooks present a very biased representation of both religion and many traditional values.

Each particular study (summarized below) was based on a careful reading of a representative sample of widely used public school textbooks. The books were read and scored by a principal investigator and then all results were verified by independent evaluators. Studies 1-5 deal with how religion and some social and political issues are represented in social studies texts for grades 1-6. Study 6 deals with the same topics as portrayed in high school American history books. Study 7 investigates how religion and certain traditional values are portrayed in readers used in grades 3 and 6.

Social Studies Textbooks, Grades 1-6: Sample Selection

The ten sets of six books used in this study were selected as follows: (1)

EDITOR'S NOTE: This essay is a summary of a more extensive report by Paul Vitz on a project funded by the National Institute of Education. Readers interested in more information about the specific public school textbooks that were sampled in this study, the methodology employed, and its more detailed findings should consult *Censorship: Evidence of Bias in Our Children's Textbooks* (Ann Arbor: Servant, 1986).

A STUDY OF PUBLIC SCHOOL TEXTBOOKS 117

All social studies texts adopted by the states of California and Texas were included. These two states were selected because of their large school-age populations and because many other states look to their adoption lists for guidance in selecting their own texts. (2) In addition, any other texts adopted by both Georgia and Florida were included.

This sample of ten sets was very representative of the nation as a whole. The estimate that the sample used here accounted for seventy percent of those used in the country seems reasonable, even conservative.

General Characteristics of the Sampled Books

All of the ten sets of books in the sample turned out to have the same general structure or format. The grade 1 texts dealt with the individual student in the family and school setting. Grade 2 texts expanded the setting, usually to include the student's neighborhood. Grade 3 texts expanded the context further to include the life of the surrounding community—the town or city. Grade 4 texts ranged yet further to include different regions of the country and in some cases of the world, amounting to something like geography texts incorporating stories about the lives of the people in various regions. All were rather similar to the *National Geographic* magazine in treatment. Those that covered regions of the world placed some emphasis on U.S. regions as well.

The books for these first four grades also treated aspects of U.S. history and world culture. Because of the homogeneity of the sets for the first four grades, we analyzed them together. The grade 5 texts were all introductions to U.S. history, and the grade 6 texts were all introductions either to world history or world cultures. Grade 5 books were analyzed separately from grade 6 books.

STUDY 1
RELIGION IN SOCIAL STUDIES TEXTBOOKS: GRADES 1-4

Scoring. References to religion in the books were scored as text items if they were made with words, and image items if they occurred in pictures. *Primary religious* references are defined as those that refer in words or pictures to religious activity such as praying, going to church, participating in a religious ceremony, giving religious instruction, or the like. *Secondary religious* references are those that refer to religion in some indirect way, such as mentioning the date a church was built, referring to a minister as part of the community, or showing a photograph of such things as a church, a scene showing Amish people riding in a buggy, or Jews by an Israeli parade float as part of a treatment of different ethnic groups in the U.S.

Reliability. The reliability of the scoring the various religious categories received was checked by having the texts analyzed by an independent scorer provided by Educational Products Information Exchange (E.P.I.E.). The summary score sheets for all books (grades 1-4) based on the observations of the principal investigator were sent to E.P.I.E., where the independent scorer noted any references to religion that had been missed by the principal investigator. There were three such independent scorers, each of whom checked the principal investigator's scoring of three or four of the ten sets of textbooks. Two of the twenty-four examples of a primary reference to religion were missed by the principal investigator. It is therefore likely that the results are based on 100 percent or close to 100 percent of all such references in the sample. Of the seventy-six secondary religious references found, fifteen were found by the outside judges—which is to say they had been missed by the principal investigator. It is unlikely that many additional secondary references were missed by both sets of judges, so we can assume that the conclusions are based on close to all such references. After the independent check, the principal investigators reviewed the findings of outside judges, including their classification of the religious items as either primary or secondary. The principal investigator and the outside judges agreed 100 percent of the time as to which of the two categories a given reference to religion belonged in.

Results. The first result was the determination that none of the books had a single *text* reference to a primary religious activity occurring in representative contemporary American life. The closest any book came was a reference to the life of the Amish—a small, rural Protestant group whose distinctive way of life has not changed in centuries and who are thus not representative of today's Protestant Christian life. Another reference appeared in a story on a Spanish urban ghetto, "El Barrio." In this story the complete relevant text read, "Religion is important for people in El Barrio. Churches have places for dances and sports events." This was not categorized as a primary reference to religion because it does not describe any actual religious activity. The text doesn't mention Christianity or Roman Catholicism, and the churches are described as places for fun and games, not as places for worship. Also, El Barrio is a somewhat special ethnic environment; it certainly is not representative of American religious life in general.

It was also found, however, that the textbooks contained a few *im-*

ages showing primary religious activity in a contemporary American setting. In the first grade texts, two images were Jewish, one was Catholic, and there was a rather vaguely drawn picture of a minister or priest at a funeral. In grade 2 texts there was one Jewish image and a photograph of a family praying at a Thanksgiving dinner (nondenominational). Primary religious images found in grade 3 texts included a Catholic priest, a rabbi, a minister or priest (with a clerical collar) at a sick bed, and a family with heads bowed for Thanksgiving. The grade 4 texts did not contain any primary religious images dealing with contemporary American society.

The secondary religious references, both text and image, presented a similar pattern.

It will be useful to get some statistical idea of how rare these few religious images actually were. In all books, the primary religious images referring to contemporary U.S. life were less frequent than one in two hundred images. For example, every book that had any reference to religion had one hundred or more pages that could have images, and yet no book had more than one U.S. primary religious image; some had no primary religious images at all. In the books for grades 1-3, there were on average about two images for every page, which means that primary religious images accounted for fewer than one in two hundred images in these books. A similar pattern held for grade 4 texts.

In short, the most striking thing about these texts was the total absence of any primary textual references to typical contemporary American religious life. Specifically, there was not one textual reference to characteristic American Protestant religious life in these books.

The situation was only slightly better with regard to primary images. There were four images referring to contemporary Jewish practice, two to contemporary Catholic life, and one to a man in clerical dress described as a minister visiting the sick. There were two figures that might have been either a priest or a minister, and there were two portraits of families whose religious affiliation was not specified bowing their heads in prayer at a Thanksgiving dinner.

Of course, in texts discussing the colonial period there were primary references in text and images to the Protestantism of the New England Puritans, but in essence these were references to something that no longer exists. Representations of the Puritan religious life are typically ambiguous for children today. In some respects such discussions convey the message that religion is old-fashioned and only for those who are not up-to-date. One text that contained a two-page story on Peacham, Vermont, set in the present describes a beautiful old "Puritan" church in this small village not as a center of religious life but as the site of a contemporary summer piano festival. The implicit message that religion is old-fashioned was also found in texts that discussed the Spanish missions and in several references to the Amish.

In any case, the principal point again is that this sample of forty social studies texts, which were ostensibly meant to introduce students to American society as it exists today (and, to a lesser extent, how it existed in the past), did not contain a single reference in word or image to today's powerful Protestant religious world of the Bible Belt, of the TV evangelists, of the born-again Christians, of the fundamentalists and the evangelicals, of the Moral Majority, of Billy Graham, Oral Roberts, Jerry Falwell, Pat Robertson—even of Norman Vincent Peale—this very American world representing millions of Americans. Nothing about the world of mainline Protestantism was acknowledged even once. The books placed a heavy emphasis instead on such things as today's job market and the world of recreation.

As we have noted, the texts do make passing references to religion without reflecting anything of its proportional significance in American life. But another imbalance is also interesting. The references that do appear tend to be images of Jewish, Catholic, and, to a lesser extent, Amish or Mormon religious life. Presumably the emphasis on these religions is part of a pro-minority bias—though even as such it is not particularly widespread among the text, and it overlooks the point that mainstream Catholics do not really constitute a religious minority. Most striking of all is the complete absence of any kind of reference to contemporary America's majority religion—Protestant Christianity. As will become clear, this failure to reflect America's majority religious tradition is echoed in the texts' treatment of the family, economic, and political traditions as well.

Because our primary concern in this study is with the ways in which U.S. life and history are represented in textbooks, we did not focus as closely on the occasional references in these books to other countries, such as Mexico and France, or to other cultural traditions, such as those of Native Americans. However, it is noteworthy that in such references to other countries and cultures, religion gets a substantially greater emphasis. For example, many of the texts treated Native American life prior to the arrival of Europeans, and they typically gave Native American religion a sympathetic treatment. One book described a Hopi rain dance and prayer; another contained a Pueblo Indian story about prayer and how the Earth Mother created corn for them.

Texts that treated Mexico usually mentioned religious matters.

One text explicitly noted "religious" celebrations, though it failed to characterize them as either Catholic or Christian. Another text referred to the "Christ of the Andes" statue in discussing South America.

One text contained the comment, "As you see, in Europe many people are religious." None of the books contained a similar statement about the United States, however, even though religion has always been central to American life.

Other examples of the way religion was washed out of these texts can be found in such remarks as "Pilgrims are people who make long trips" and "Mardi Gras is the end of winter celebration" and in the fact that these books include significant discussions of such American cities as San Francisco, Santa Fe, St. Paul, St. Louis, and St. Augustine without giving any indication of who the cities are named after.

In sum, then, it seems that it is considered acceptable to mention America's less "typical" religions in textbooks, but mainstream Protestantism is for all practical purposes considered taboo. The effect of this is a denial of the fact that religion is really an important part of American life. Sometimes the censorship becomes especially offensive. One book, for example, devoted thirty pages to a discussion of the Pilgrims, noting that they celebrated Thanksgiving because they "wanted to give thanks for all they had"—and yet it nowhere specifies that it was God that they were offering their thanks to. This sort of thing occurred again and again in the sample texts. It is permissible to refer to the Pueblo Indians praying to Mother Earth, but Pilgrims can't be described as praying to God.

STUDY 2
RELIGION IN THE INTRODUCTION TO AMERICAN HISTORY
TEXTBOOKS: SOCIAL STUDIES, GRADE 5

The grade 5 textbooks from all ten publishers were introductions to U.S. history. Some books also included material on Mexican and Canadian history, but we did not focus on this because we were principally concerned with how religion is represented in *American* history. The only possibly ambiguous religious reference with respect to American history involved Hitler's persecution of the Jews. Although this event is, strictly speaking, primarily German and European in character, the effects the Holocaust had on American life render it a special aspect of American history.

Scoring. Every page of every book was read, and a brief summary of any reference to religion was made. Initially every reference was also scored as expressing a positive, negative, or neutral attitude toward religion. Since most of the references were neutral, no regular attempt was made to treat this aspect of references to religion. Instead we primarily concerned ourselves with the issue of whether religion was mentioned and what characteristics were represented when it was.

General Discussion. The overwhelming impression that arose from our analysis of all these books was the superficiality of their treatment of just about everything. They generally amounted to a pastiche of topics and images without any serious historical treatment of what might have been going on. Nevertheless, certain aspects of the coverage of religion deserve special emphasis.

1. Not one book noted the extreme liveliness and great importance of religion for American life—the sort of religious energy expressed in the development of such groups as the Shakers, the Mormons, Christian Scientists, Jehovah's Witnesses, Seventh-day Adventists, and Black Muslims, among many others.

2. There was not one reference in any of these books to such important religious events as the Salem witch trials, the Great Awakening of the 1740s, the great revivals of the 1830s and 1840s, the great urban revivals of the 1870-1890 period, the very important Holiness and Pentecostal movements that sprang up around 1880 to 1910, the split between liberal and conservative Protestants that took place early in the twentieth century, or the born-again movement of the 1960s and '70s. In short, religion in the twentieth century hardly figures at all in these books.

3. In spite of the emphasis on religious freedom and tolerance in these books, there was not one reference to the Catholic school system or to the recent Christian school movement as an expression of religious freedom.

Frequency of Reference to Religion. As noted earlier, all references to religion in the texts in our sampling that dealt with the history of the United States (or the history of the territories that became part of it) were recorded on summary data sheets. The relevant historical events were grouped for each text by centuries, starting with the 1600s, in order to give an indication of the relative significance accorded to religious issues in the various time periods being discussed. The results indicate, for example, that the average text had 24.5 pages covering the history of the 1600s and that slightly more than fifty percent of these pages contained some reference to religion. The comparable figure for the pages covering the 1700s was 9.75 percent, and for the 1800s it was 3.42 percent. For the 1900s the frequency of appearance dropped to just 1.27 references for every hundred pages. (References to the Jewish Holocaust in Nazi Germany were not included in the latter figure; they are, however, noted and discussed below.)

Judaism. The treatment of Judaism in these books is spotty. Jewish aspects of U.S. history have been important, but, like those of many religious groups, they are not generally well known. We established five categories of significant Jewish aspects of U.S. history in our attempt to measure how well Judaism is represented in these books: (1) the presence of Jews in America in the seventeenth and eighteenth centuries; (2) Jewish immigration into the United States from 1880 to 1920; (3) the existence of anti-Jewish prejudice in the country, such as that from the Ku Klux Klan; (4) the significance of the Nazi Holocaust in World War II; and (5) any other reference. As noted earlier, the Nazi Holocaust is not part of American history per se, but we included it because of its intrinsic significance and because of its effects on much of U.S. religious and political life. We scored each of the ten books in the sample on its inclusion of items in the five categories. One book contained material that fell into all five categories; four texts contained material in only one.

Catholicism. The specific treatment of American Roman Catholicism is, if anything, weaker than the coverage of Jewish American contributions. Eight major Catholic aspects of U.S. history were singled out in our study to measure how well Catholic contributions were represented in sampled textbooks: (1) the very significant early Catholic settling of Florida, the Southwest, and California; (2) the Catholic presence in colonial America; (3) the intense anti-Catholic prejudice in the period from 1830 to 1865; (4) the establishment of the Catholic school system as a major expression of religious freedom; (5) the role of the Roman Catholic Church in assimilating large numbers of immigrants from Ireland, Italy, Germany, Poland, and Lithuania; (6) the very large number of Catholic hospitals, schools, orphanages, and the like; (7) the anti-Catholic prejudice in twentieth-century America, as expressed by the KKK and in the presidential elections involving Al Smith and John F. Kennedy; and (8) interesting and important Catholic personalities, such as Lord Baltimore, Elizabeth Seton, Orestes Brownson, Isaac Hecker, Mother Cabrini, and others.

The coverage of Catholic contributions to U.S. history can be described very simply. All of the texts in the sample had references (usually not extensive) to material in the first two categories, involving the period of the 1700s or earlier, but beyond this only two books made any sort of reference to anything that could be placed in the remaining six categories. A McGraw Hill text referred to anti-Catholic prejudice in mid-nineteenth-century America, and a Holt text referred to such prejudice in twentieth-century America (e.g., from the KKK). Apart from these two references, the texts in the sample simply excluded Catholicism from U.S. history from 1800 to the present. That the Catholic school system was founded at great cost and sacrifice as an expression of the American search for religious freedom is not mentioned once, despite the fact that the issue of religious freedom explains most of the references to religion in American colonial history. This oversight might be attributable to anti-Catholic prejudice on the part of the authors of the textbooks, though it probably makes better sense to attribute it to the fact that the present public school monopoly tends to exclude all such references to alternative systems. Perhaps such exclusions are an expression of concern that new Protestant schools using the same religious freedom rationale have siphoned off thousands of public school students in the last twenty years as Protestants have sought to pass on their faith and moral traditions to their children.

STUDY 3
RELIGION IN WORLD HISTORY AND WORLD CULTURES TEXTBOOKS: GRADE 6

The ten grade 6 social studies texts in the sample we studied all briefly covered either world history or world cultures with history mixed in. Because these books differed in the particular historical periods, countries, and cultures they covered, it was difficult to compare them systematically. Nevertheless we did find evidence of bias in their coverage of Judaism and Christianity.

Scoring. Each page of each book was read and any reference to religion was briefly summarized. The results indicated a relative neglect of a number of important topics.

1. *Ancient Jewish History.* The early history of the Jews is of foundational significance to the West. In many respects it is as important as the history of the ancient Greeks and more important than that of the ancient Egyptians. However there is far less coverage of Jewish history than of either Egyptian or Greek history in most of these books. Certainly the origin of monotheism and the stories of Abraham, Moses, David, and such prophets as Isaiah and Jeremiah are central to Western life and history as well as to much of Islam. Although some of these people and topics are mentioned, on the whole they get little emphasis. Moreover, none of the texts in the sample made any reference to Jewish

life and culture during the period between the death of Christ and the Holocaust. In other words, the Judeo- part of the West's Judeo-Christian heritage was far from adequately represented in these texts.

2. *The Life of Jesus of Nazareth*. Whatever one thinks of Christianity, it has certainly been of central importance in world history, and the life of Jesus of Nazareth is in turn crucial to the story of Christianity. Indeed, many claim that his life is the most important single historical event in the past two thousand years. Certainly the history of Europe, the Americas, and much of the Near East, Africa, and even Asia cannot be understood without reference to his life and what it has meant—for good or ill—for countless others. Yet none of these books treated the life of Jesus as anything like an event of this stature. A few of the books gave him some coverage, but four mentioned nothing at all about his life or teaching. Others gave so little as to be banal. For example, one summarized Jesus' life in just three sentences: "Jesus became a teacher. He preached that there was only One God. He told those who would listen that they must honor God by treating others with love and forgiveness." Besides the trivialization in this description, it has one major error. Jesus did not make a point of preaching that there was "only One God." Monotheism was assumed in Jewish life, and Jesus gave it little direct attention per se. In fact the phrase "only One God" is central to Islam, not Christianity.

The extent to which the texts in the sample neglected the life of Jesus is yet more startling in light of the amount of material some of them devote to describing the life of Mohammed. One text described the life of Jesus in the space of 36 lines while devoting 104 lines to the life of Mohammed. Another mentioned Mohammed as founder of Islam but did not make a single reference to Jesus in any context. Yet another included an eleven-page section as well as other scattered coverage to the rise of Islam, Islamic culture, and Mohammed while discussing the rise of Christianity in just a few lines on a single page. It is not that the books in the sample avoided discussion of great religious figures entirely; they simply avoided discussion of Jesus.

3. *The First Thousand Years of Christianity*. Most of the texts dealing with world history covered ancient Rome, and these typically made some reference to the fact that Christianity spread late in the history of the Empire. The end of Rome marked the end of a section in these books, and in most of them it was followed by a section dealing with the rise of Islam. In most texts the section on Islam was followed by a treatment of the Middle Ages. Thus, the texts in the sample placed very little emphasis on the first thousand years of Christianity while giv-

ing considerable attention to the rise of Islam. Only the McGraw-Hill text had a significant section on the rise of Christianity and the first centuries of the church.

4. *Eastern Orthodox Christianity and the Byzantine Empire.* With one or two exceptions, the world of Byzantium was either not mentioned at all or seriously neglected. This failing is of course related in part to the general neglect of the first thousand years of Christian history. Only two texts gave even modest coverage to the Eastern Orthodox world and culture. Three books had no textual references to Eastern Orthodoxy (or Byzantium) at all.

5. *Protestantism.* It was very strange to find that many of the texts either gave very little emphasis to the Protestant Reformation or failed to mention it entirely. One book not only failed to mention the Reformation but scarcely made any mention of Protestantism. Another devoted twenty pages to Tanzania, nineteen pages to the Netherlands, and sixteen pages to ancient Crete but made no reference to Martin Luther or John Calvin and said virtually nothing about Protestantism. The absence of references to Protestantism in Holland is particularly noteworthy given that country's history. And, incredibly, even the texts that did discuss the Reformation largely failed to go into the theological differences that were at issue. One text mentioned Martin Luther breaking away from the Catholic Church but cited no reason of any kind for the break. Only two of the texts referred to plausible religious reasons for the Reformation, and one of these did so only incidentally.

6. *Christianity in the Modern World.* None of the texts in the sample gave much emphasis at all to Christianity as a living cultural and historical force during the past two hundred years, especially in the U.S. This was particularly noticeable in view of the fact that they tended to give religion a significant place in their discussions of life in many other modern cultures. None of them described the Arab world, for example, without a serious treatment of Islam. Some took special note of such things as the religious aspects of the conflict in Northern Ireland and the importance of Catholicism in South American societies. On the whole, the relative absence of references to religion in the United States in this sample of textbooks mirrors that in the samples for grades 1-4 and 5.

In addition to these points about the presence of religious references in the books in this sample, our analysis also turned up a feminist emphasis that was projected back onto historical events. Influential women of the past were mentioned or even featured all out of proportion to their historical significance. For example, one book mentioned that Muslims kept women out of power but then featured the one known sultanate of a Muslim woman (it lasted four years). A particularly disturbing example of this emphasis turned up in one textbook that told the story of Joan of Arc without making any reference at all to God, to religion, or to the fact that she was a saint. This entirely secular account was apparently included in the text solely because Joan of Arc was a woman.

STUDY 4
FAMILY VALUES IN SOCIAL STUDIES TEXTBOOKS: GRADES 1-4

This study addressed the ways in which the family and family values were treated in social studies texts.

Sample and Scoring. The social studies texts for grades 5 and 6 addressed U.S. history and world history and culture and so they were excluded from this sample as being essentially irrelevant to the issue of family values. Hence the sample included only the books for grades 1-4—books purporting to introduce the child to an understanding of U.S. society.

Each page of the books in the sample that referred to a family, to family life, or a member of family (e.g., father, mother, aunt) was scored as having a "family" emphasis.

Results. The individual books varied greatly in the nature of their emphasis on family, although in general most contained a significant emphasis in this area. The serious issues, then, involve the kind of emphasis they presented—matters of quality rather than mere quantity. One key issue is the way the books defined the family. One text stated simply that "A family is a group of people." The teacher's edition of this book elaborated the definition to the extent of suggesting that a family is a group of people "who identify themselves as family members." In addition to providing this sort of subjective definition of the family, each of the books in the sample put a special emphasis on the idea that there are many types of families—with the implication that all are equally legitimate.

The family was most commonly defined as "the people you live with," but more often the texts provided no explicit definition. Instead, pictures and stories referring to family life built up an implicit definition. In these cases, the images tended to suggest that a family consists of those people, whoever they might be, that the child lives with. Families were variously depicted as a mother and children without a father (this grouping was notably prominent), a father and children without a mother, a couple without children, and so on.

More importantly, basic ideas with respect to the nature of the family were entirely excluded from these texts. None of the books referred to marriage as the foundation of the family. Indeed, the words *marriage* and *wedding* did not appear in any of the forty books in the sample—with one exception: one book referred to a neighbor's wedding, but this occurred in a short treatment of life in Spain. Nor were the words *husband* or *wife* found in any of the books. The fact that marriage is so pointedly removed from the definition of the family would seem to amount to a clear example of ideological bias.

Basic family values were also noticeably absent from the books in the sample. Not one of the many families described in these books featured a homemaker—that is, a wife and mother who chooses not to work outside the home. The words *housewife* and *homemaker* did not appear anywhere in the books, although there were a large number of references to mothers and other women in such occupations as medicine, transportation, and politics. None of the books suggested that the occupation of homemaker is important, that one could pursue the occupation with integrity, or that it might provide any sort of satisfaction. In the entire sample there was one story in which the mother presumably was a mother and housewife, but this wasn't made explicit in any way. In general, traditional family sex roles were represented infrequently, and only in the context of family life in the historic past or in other countries. There was not one portrayal of a contemporary American family that clearly featured traditional sex roles.

STUDY 5
OTHER OBSERVATIONS ON SOCIAL STUDIES TEXTBOOKS: GRADES 1-4

In the course of reading these books, certain observations were made that had not been anticipated.

A Strong Partisan Political Emphasis. There was a clear partisan political character of a liberal bent to the social studies texts in this sample. Many of the books singled out certain prominent people for special emphasis. These people were not necessary for the discussion of social life or the history of the United States (as, for instance, presidents would be) but were included as significant individuals who would interest the students. There is evidence that they were meant to serve as "role models" for the students in the fact that they were usually featured under such headings as "Famous People," "Someone You Should Know," "People Who Made a Difference," and the like. Special emphasis was placed on people who have made major contributions after World War II—that is, contemporary political role models.

A person was scored as a political "role model" if he or she was singled out for distinctive biographical treatment and if the person was active in political life or well-known for his or her political or ideological significance, such as Martin Luther King, Jr. People selected as role models in the arts, from sports, and from the world of science were not included in this analysis. Only those individuals who were named, whose pictures appeared in the text, and whose lives or accomplishments received special treatment (at least a paragraph or a page in length) were included in the scoring.

The substantial liberal bias of these selections is as much evidenced by a list of those who are not profiled as by a list of those who are. Among those not selected are General Douglas MacArthur, Robert A. Taft, Barry Goldwater, William Buckley, Jesse Helms, Jack Kemp, Billy Graham, Jerry Falwell, neo-conservatives such as Irving Kristol, and the whole of the youthful group of business entrepreneurs behind today's high tech businesses. Indeed, not only do the books fail to feature the Silicon Valley phenomenon but they fail to feature any business executive active since World War II as a role model. Similarly omitted are such conservative women as Nellie Gray, Phyllis Schlafly, and Jeanne Kirkpatrick. For a list of those who were selected, see Table 1 on page 130.

The generally liberal credentials of those listed in Table 1 make clear the political agenda in these books. There are few Republican role models—the exceptions being Milicent Fenwick, a liberal pro-abortion, pro-ERA congresswoman; Nancy Kassebaum, a moderate Republican; and Clare Booth Luce, a conservative Republican and an ambassador active thirty years ago. The list suggests there haven't been any male Republicans in the country or indeed any active conservatives male or female during the past twenty years—and this despite the striking political ascendancy of conservatives in recent years. In any case, it is clear that the textbooks in the sample are presenting a disproportionately large number of liberals and a disproportionately small number of conservatives as role models for the children in the public school system.

Political bias was also evident in the tendency of these books to reliably characterize recent and much of past U.S. history in terms of certain themes. All of the textbooks in the sample advocated minority

Table 1

All people of post–World War II political and social significance selected for special biographical emphasis (role models) in the Social Studies Texts: Grades 1-6. See text for details of selection.

Name	Party	Accomplishment	Publisher-Grade
Herman Badillo	Dem.	N.Y. City politician	Holt-4
Romana Banuelos	Dem.	Treasurer of U.S.	Laidlaw-1
Thomas Bradley (2 times)	Dem.	Mayor of Los Angeles	Holt-4; McGraw-3
Ralph Bunche	Dem.	United Nations Offic.	Amer/Heath-4
Rachel Carson (2 times)	N.A.	Ecology movement	Holt-1; Amer/Heath-4
Raul Castro	Dem.	Gov. of Arizona	Laidlaw-5
Henry Cisneros	Dem.	Mayor of San Antonio	Scott-Fores.-4
Vine DeLoria	N.A.	Amer. Indian rights	Laidlaw-1
Millicent Fenwick	Rep.	U.S. Congress, N.J.	Follett 4
Ella Grasso	Dem.	Gov. of Connecticut	Scott-Fores.-4
Patricia Harris	Dem.	Lawyer; black rights	Holt-4
Dolores Huerta	N.A.	United Farm Workers	Scott-Fores.-3
Nancy Kassebaum	Rep.	U.S. Senate, Kansas	Laidlaw-2
Maggie Kuhn	N.A.	Gray Panthers/Feminist	Amer/Heath-4
Martin L. King, Jr. (3 times)	N.A.	Civil rights leader	Laidlaw-1; Holt-4; Silver-Bur.-4
Clare Booth Luce	Rep.	Ambassador	Laidlaw-1
Thurgood Marshall	N.A.	Supreme Court Justice	Laidlaw-2
Margaret Mead (2 times)	N.A.	Anthropologist	Holt-6; Amer/Heath-4
Patsy Mink	Dem.	U.S. Congress, Hawaii	Holt-4
Julian Nava	Dem.	Ambass to Mex; author	Amer/Heath-4
Dixie Lee Ray	Dem.	Gov of Washington	Amer/Heath-4
Eleanor Roosevelt (3 times)	Dem.	Founder of UN; various good works	Holt-4; Scholas-6; Scott-Fores.-4
Coleman Young	Dem.	Mayor, Detroit	Scott-Fores.-3

rights, feminism, and ecology and environmental issues without giving any serious consideration to alternative—specifically conservative—views. For example, they made no mention of the anti-ERA movement, the pro-life movement, or the tax revolt.

A Money and Career Emphasis. All of the texts in the sample presented work as having two primary ends. The first is to get paid money that can be used to buy goods to satisfy needs and wants. A typical treatment showed a man or woman—explicitly or implicitly a father or mother—working at some job, getting paid, and then going to the store to buy something. The second end of work is to gain status, as in a career. Although it was not mentioned in the text, the images tended to convey the idea that work is a relatively pleasant or satisfying activity in its own right. It was certainly not presented as drudgery.

However, there was not one mention in any of the texts of the fact that many people work for rewards other than money—people such as homemakers, for instance, and those who volunteer their services to hospitals and other organizations. Many people exchange goods and services—barter—to support themselves. And many others—presumably people such as school teachers—are paid money for the work they do but have chosen their jobs in part for the rewards other than money that they receive. None of the texts in the sample spoke of people regularly working out of concern for others or because of the intrinsic value of certain kinds of work. The absence of any concern for nonmaterial values was also pointedly apparent in the discussions of the family budget that appeared in the text: none of these discussions spoke of setting aside any money for charity, for others in need, or for giving to a church. The emphasis remained uniformly on personal status and enjoyment and the money economy. The implicit message was clear: if you work and don't get paid money, you—and what you do—don't really count.

STUDY 6
U.S. HISTORY TEXTBOOKS: GRADES 11 AND 12

This study investigated the ways in which religion was represented in the U.S. history textbooks used throughout the country in the eleventh and twelfth grades.

Sample. Fourteen states provided us with lists of the U.S. history textbooks that had been adopted for the eleventh and twelfth grades in their school systems. From these lists we determined that twelve textbooks had been adopted by five or more states. These books were judged as representative. From this list of twelve, we selected eight texts at random. This sample of eight books was highly representative of the country: we estimated that close to 60 percent of the country's eleventh and twelfth graders taking U.S. history used one of the books in the sample.

Scoring. Scorers read each page of each book in the sample and noted all references to religion. Since each text had at least a moderately thorough index, the scorers also noted all index entries relating to religion. All of the scoring for each book was independently verified by an outside scorer supplied by E.P.I.E. This outside scorer turned up references that the principal investigators had missed in the amount of about 10 percent of the totals. The general summaries that follow are based on the complete list of references found by both the principal investigator and the E.P.I.E. scorer. The summaries were also evaluated for accuracy by an E.P.I.E. scorer. Although an occasional reference to religion may have been missed, it is most unlikely that any important treatment was overlooked.

General Description. On average the books in this sample were twice as long as the fifth grade texts, running to seven or eight hundred pages; they also had more words per page, fewer photos, and fewer exercises. As a consequence these books had at least three or four times more coverage of American history than the fifth grade social studies books. They were all written in a much more scholarly way, some of them by quite prominent American historians. So, overall the books were much more substantial than the texts for the lower grades. The authors presumably represented a much higher level of competence—in some cases the very highest level of historical scholarship in the country. We expected a great deal more of these texts than we did of the grade 5 social studies books.

Results. Not one of these texts recognized, much less emphasized, the great religious energy and creativity of the U.S. None of the books provided any serious coverage of conservative Protestantism in the past hundred years, although a few them mentioned the Scopes trial. None of them mentioned the many evangelical movements that have arisen during the past hundred years. Very simply, these history texts made no effort to discuss the heritage and history of tens of millions of American Christians.

The books in the sample contained other more specific flaws as well. None of them gave evidence of any serious appreciation of Catholic contributions to American life. Most of the texts contained some discussion of prejudice against Catholics, but with one minor exception there was no mention in any of them of such things as the assimilation of countless immigrants into Catholic communities, the many hospitals and orphanages built by Catholics, or the significance of the Catholic school system. The contributions of American Jews similarly received little notice.

Even many of the "standard" religious aspects or events of American history were often left out of those books. For example, many failed to mention one (or both) of the Great Awakenings, the Salem witch trials, and the deep links between various Christian denominations and the anti-slavery movement. One index to the abysmal treatment of religion in American history was the universal tendency to list the dates of important historical events and to leave out from such lists almost all dates referring to religion, especially in the past hundred years.

One additional characteristic of these texts was their tendency to omit conservative political issues and conservative historical figures in presenting U.S. history since World War II.

STUDY 7
RELIGION AND OTHER VALUES IN READERS: GRADES 3 AND 6

This study investigated how religion and other values were represented in the books used to teach reading. These books—known as basal readers—primarily use stories (typically fiction, but nature, science, and biographical pieces as well) to develop students' reading ability. The content of these stories and articles is an important source of values and information for students.

Sample. Eleven texts used as readers for grade 3 and eleven texts used as readers for grade 6 were selected for study. All of them were on the official adoption list of either California or Texas and hence constituted a very representative sample of texts used generally throughout the United States.

Scoring. Only stories or articles were scored. Poems, plays, games, exercises, reviews, and similar material were not evaluated. They never accounted for more than a relatively small part of the total content of any book in any case; stories and articles usually took up anywhere from 75 to 90 percent of the pages. The stories and articles included ordinary and historical fiction, factual material (e.g., a nature article), and the sort of mixture of fact and fiction that characterized most of the biographies in these readers. Scoring consisted of brief written summaries by the principal investigator or an assistant on each story and article in each book. All references to religion were specifically noted. The principal investigator subsequently read all the stories and articles that had been scored by the assistant to gain firsthand familiarity with the complete sample.

An independent analyst read all the stories in four randomly selected texts to check on the accuracy of the principal investigator's summaries. This analyst found only one story out of 140 that had a reference to religion of any significance that was missed by the principal investigator—the phrase "good Lord" used in one sentence. We assumed then, that although a few stray religious references might have been missed in the sample, it was not likely that such oversights would change any of the major conclusions. In addition, all of our conclusions and results were evaluated for accuracy by the independent evaluator.

General Character of the Stories. The overwhelming majority of these stories and articles were the literary equivalent of elevator music: lightweight, sentimental, and not very challenging. The simple topics and the simple vocabulary of the pieces were very much the same from one text to another. There was in fact little to distinguish one grade 3 book from another. All in all, they amounted to about equal mixtures of pap and propaganda.

Treatment of Religion. For all intents and purposes religion was absent from the sample's basal readers. There was not one story or article in all these books in which the central motivation or major content involved religion. No character had a primary religious motivation, and religious motivation was a secondary concern in only five or six stories or articles. Beyond this, religion entered some stories in a minor or peripheral way, but without any narrative importance.

No informative article dealt with religion as a primary subject worthy of treatment. There were scores of articles about animals, archaeology, fossils, and magic but none on religion, much less about Christianity. In contrast to the serious neglect of Christianity and Judaism, there was a minor spiritual or occult emphasis in a number of stories about Native Americans. One fifty-five-page story featured a typical white American girl on a ranch in California who sought ways to commune with animal spirits as part of her search for her "Indian Heart." She made several animal fetishes and believed that they captured the spirit of an animal, such as a coyote. Another story called "Medicine Bag" featured an Indian medicine bag passed on from father to son as part of the Indian youth's "vision quest," in which he sought out the meaning of his name. An article about Comanche medicine art gave information about Native American spirituality in addition to providing an interpretation of an artist's paintings. This article also made some misleading comparisons between biblical beliefs and Native American spirituality, as in the statement that "A prophet [in the Bible] was said to have come from another world, or Heaven, to give People on Earth vision, or a reason for being. . . . People you call saints or disciples wrote down what they 'saw' through your prophets." This suggestion that the Bible teaches that prophets come from another world constitutes a serious misrepresentation of the Judeo-Christian concept of a prophet. If the author was referring to Jesus as a prophet, that would raise even more disturbing issues.

Among the stories with secondary religious references there was something of a small Roman Catholic theme. A biography of the Mayo brothers and their establishment of the Mayo Clinic mentioned that an order of Catholic nuns was instrumental in setting up the Mayos' first hospital, called St. Mary's. A story featuring Joliet and Marquette mentioned that the latter was a Catholic priest. A story on the animals of China mentioned a French priest-naturalist, Fr. David. Another story mentioned a Hispanic artist who among other things drew a nativity scene. An article on masks mentioned masks in South American religious festivals and identified Mardi Gras and Lent. In a story about the famous battle at the Alamo, the structure was described as a mission church in Texas, a young boy referred to his family's church and to Our Lady of Guadalupe, and the boy's mother prayed for the safety of her Hispanic husband, the boy's father, during the battle. Of course, even in these pieces the quantity of religious references was small and the references were almost wholly descriptive, having no clear religious content. Only the Mayo story and story about the Alamo contained primary religious references (e.g., the reference to the mother praying and the son's comment about Our Lady of Guadalupe), but the significance of the actions being referred to was somewhat ambiguous (e.g., the mother's prayers were ineffectual; her husband was killed along with the rest of the defenders). All other religious references in the sample were merely secondary.

A story by the Jewish writer Isaac Bashevis Singer set in the nineteenth century in a small village in Eastern Europe had something of a religious theme. The story takes place at Hanukkah and involves a Jewish boy who gets lost for three days in a blizzard with the family goat. He is saved by finding a haystack in which to sit out the storm with the goat, who keeps him warm and supplies milk. After the storm he returns home. At one point in the story he prays, though God's name is not mentioned. The celebration of Hanukkah provides an important context for the story, but its religious and political meanings are not explained, and for most readers it will probably have no more signficance than if it were any unnamed ethnic holiday.

There was also a brief selection from a story about two Jewish girls hidden in the home of a Dutch farmer. Except for the initial identification of the girls as Jewish, however, there was no reference to religion.

Another story centered on the mother in a Jewish household making gefilte fish (from a live carp kept in the bathtub) for Passover. God is mentioned once in the story, but no reference is made to the religious meaning of Passover. Indeed, the focus of the article is on the poor fish. Like Hanukkah in the previously mentioned story, Passover is no more significant in this story than a strictly secular ethnic holiday would be for the purpose of the text.

Religion was also referred to in a neutral or a strongly positive fashion in a few stories on black history and black life. And the preface to one piece explained that it was about a Mennonite family in America that had fled Russia to avoid religious persecution. A story about pioneer life on the prairie described Christmas as a warm time when people prepared special foods. This is really not a religious reference since the text describes Christmas as no more than a time for "thought and thanksgiving" without referring to any religious meaning. And one piece about King Arthur referred to the Bible, a cathedral, and an archbishop.

In all these examples we found the same pattern established in the social studies textbooks: (1) there was no major Christian or Jewish religious motivation at all and almost no serious representation of religion, (2) there were no references to typical active Protestantism, but a small number of "minority" religions (e.g., Catholic, Jewish, black, Mennonite) did get some clear positive representation, and (3) the few references to religion are mostly descriptive and neutral—that is, secondary religious references. For example, even in a relatively religious biographical piece on Martin Luther King, Jr., there was no reference to how Christian ideas or the life of Jesus affected him. (As was the case in all the social studies and history texts we examined, the name "Jesus" didn't occur anywhere in these books.)

Besides the examples already noted, two stories contained single references to a major character praying at a time of extreme danger. One involved two boys who thought they were lost on an ice floe and the other involved a boat carrying immigrants from Ireland that had trouble in a storm. No reference was made to how or to whom they prayed, however. And finally there was another story in which a man rescued after days of living alone on a large iceberg expressed his delight at being rescued by shouting "Gott im Himmel."

A few of the pieces contained references to God or Christianity that were negative or so neutral as to be implicitly negative. For example, one book included a story about Maria Mitchell, an astronomer in nineteenth-century America who visited the Vatican observatory. The piece had a strong feminist message as well as some comments that referred somewhat critically to Christianity in the context of the trial of Galileo. This story also referred to "the Book of Nature and the Book of God," implying that nature is not also the book of God.

Religions other than Christianity and Judaism were mentioned more frequently. There were references to Greek and Roman religion in six stories, references to ancient Egyptian, Polynesian, and other pagan religions in six stories, and two not especially religious stories were attributed to Buddha. Native American religion was featured quite positively in five stories and one article. But none of the books in the sample contained any Bible stories—not even such familiar accounts as that of David and Goliath.

Other biases in these 670 stories and articles relevant to the present study are also noteworthy.

1. *Lack of Patriotism*. There were only five stories in these books with any sort of patriotic theme. Three of them told the story of Sybil Ludington, who in 1777 dressed as a man and rode about the countryside warning local pro-independence farmers about a British threat. This feminist counterpart to the story of Paul Revere's ride had little of a specifically patriotic character about it. There was also a story about Mary, a black girl who wanted to join the army and who helped bring food to George Washington's troops during the harsh winter at Valley Forge. The fifth story was about an American boy who during the Revolutionary War captured a British soldier who had been stealing vegetables from his garden.

In general, then, the study indicated that of the twenty-two books in the sample, seventeen (over 75 percent) did not contain any patriotic stories. Furthermore, none of the patriotic stories that did appear in the sample had anything to do with American history during the past two hundred years. Four of the five stories featured girls and might better be described as feminist than patriotic in orientation.

2. *Lack of Support for Business*. There were only five pieces that could be described as having a business theme. One was about a boy who ran a baby-sitting service, although the story centered on the silly events that took place one night he spent sleeping out in a tent with a

young boy he was "babysitting." Another was an article about a black youth who bought a house in a run-down part of town, fixed it up, and became the youngest landlord in Michigan. Here, the emphasis was on good citizenship—and on making it as a young black—rather than on business success. The remaining pieces were all about Maggie Mitchell Walker, a black woman from Richmond, Virginia, born in 1867, who became a successful banker. This story—the only true business success story in the sample—appeared in three different readers. The major emphasis of the stories in all three texts, however, was on the feminist issue rather than on business; the focus was on her accomplishment in overcoming prejudice against women rather than on her triumph in the business community per se. The racial issue was not significant in the story because all of the characters were black.

In the whole sample there were no stories about Henry Ford, Andrew Carnegie, or any more recent figures in the world of business. Nor was there a single story in which an immigrant to this country found happiness and success in business or in a profession. As in the social studies texts, individuals such as Lee Iacocca and An Wang are as much excluded as their out-of-favor predecessor Horatio Alger. And no more attention is paid to representatives of labor and labor unions than is given to management figures.

In conclusion, then, the texts in the sample grossly underrepresented this country's workers and particularly our entrepreneurial business spirit. Indeed, they contained not a single word about those Americans who have built and are still building our major industries and businesses.

3. *A Feminist Emphasis.* By far the most noticeable ideological position in the readers was feminist. This emphasis was evident in a number of ways—as much in the sorts of things that were excluded from the stories and articles as what was included. For example, none of the pieces presented motherhood or marriage as a positive goal or as a rich and meaningful way of living. No story showed any woman or girl in a positive relationship with a baby or young child; no story included a girl who enjoyed having a doll; none of the books even contained a picture of a girl with a baby or a doll.

Romance also received short shrift. Only five stories focused on romance. One involved two dogs. One was an O. Henry story about a young man and a young woman who have fallen out over a misunderstanding that the story resolves. A third story featured a young black girl who daydreams that a popular singer will fall in love with her. In the fourth story a loving prince won the hand of a princess even though she had apparently changed into a cat. And the fifth story centered on the efforts of the wife of a captured Confederate officer to rescue him from prison. Dressed as a man, the woman almost succeeds, but in the end the officer is killed and she is caught and hanged. Her ghost is said to still haunt the area. The emphasis is more on her daring attempt to rescue her husband than it is on romance. Great literature, from Shakespeare to Jane Austen to Louisa May Alcott is filled with romance and the desire to marry, but one finds very little of that in these texts.

Some of the pieces were role-reversal romances of sorts. For example, there was the story of a princess who set out to slay the dragon in her kingdom. She invented the first gun and used it to shoot and kill the dragon. The slain dragon turned into a prince who asked her to marry him. She rather casually agreed—on the condition that her new kingdom would have lots of dragons in it for her to slay and lots of drawbridges for her to fix. She wanted to keep busy at such things. There were no stories in any of the texts about a prince rescuing a princess or slaying a dragon.

Stories set in the past featuring sex-role reversal and mockery of traditional stories about kings and queens and young men rescuing maidens were surprisingly common. Examples include "The Queen Who Changed Places with the King," "The Practical Princess," "The Queen Who Couldn't Bake Gingerbread," "Castle under the Sea," "The Last of the Dragons," "The Princess and the Admiral," and "Trouble in Camelot." The last three stories were especially hostile toward men and male roles.

The sample contained many stories of women who achieved success in traditionally male activities. There were many stories about women fliers, including Amelia Earhart and Harriet Quimby, but only one story about the Wright brothers, and it was only one page in length. There were no pieces about Charles Lindberg or any other male aviation pioneers. The stories about women pilots used such words as *courage*, *daring*, and the like—vocabulary largely absent from the pieces about men.

There were also explicitly feminist stories such as those about leaders in the women's movement including Elizabeth Blackwell (the first female M.D.), Elizabeth Cady Stanton, and others. These stories were much more factual than the feminist fiction pieces and addressed an important historical movement. They were honest and straightforward in their purpose, and in this they contrast sharply with the manipulative, wish-fulfillment quality of the many other feminist stories and articles.

Other feminist fiction included (1) a story about a new kid on the block who won a game of "king of the hill" and other similar activities but then turned out to be a girl, (2) a story entitled "Trail Boss" about a girl in charge of a longhorn cattle drive from Texas to Illinois (a piece that appeared in two readers), (3) a story about a dogsled race between a girl and a boy in which the girl turns back to rescue the boy when he gets in trouble and still manages to beat him to the finish line, and (4) a story about a star baseball player—a girl—who is in a hitting slump because her favorite "Rusty McGraw" bat is missing. Her friend, a girl detective, solves the problem by finding that a boy has stolen it so he could make the first team instead of the girl. In the end she gets her bat back and hits two home runs. There were many other feminist stories as well, but these story lines are representative.

There were other types of feminist bias in these books, such as stories that misrepresented history by referring to women judges, merchants, and soldiers at times and places where in fact there weren't any. In one astonishing instance, a mystery story featuring Encyclopedia Brown, a boy detective in a series of stories that are popular with children, was rewritten changing the Encyclopedia character to a girl. We found that some kind of feminist emphasis characterized approximately 10 percent of the stories and articles in the sample—sixty-five to seventy pieces overall—and the bias was especially heavy-handed in at least forty of them.

Conclusion. Our survey of the total sample of 670 pieces in these basal readers produced several notable results. First, we found no references to serious religious motivation in any of the pieces. There were few references to Christianity or Judaism of any sort, and those that we did find were typically superficial. In particular, we found virtually no mention at all of Protestantism, and especially white Protestants. Patriotism was close to nonexistent in the sample, as was appreciation of business successes. Traditional roles for both men and women received virtually no support; indeed, there was an implicit criticism of such roles in the many feminist stories and articles that described women engaged in activities that have traditionally belonged to men. Clear attacks on both traditional sex roles and more especially traditional concepts of manhood were common.

Altogether, the basal readers in the sample, like the social studies texts we examined, clearly represented a systematic denial of the history, heritage, beliefs, and values of a very large segment of the American people.

The Story of an Encounter

Tracy Early

When participants gathered for the conference on "Democracy and the Renewal of Public Education," they had in mind a broader than usual definition of "public." To them it meant all schooling designed to serve the people, whether administered by government authorities, religious bodies, or any other bodies.

They seemed generally agreed, too, that public education needed renewal in some rather fundamental sense and that this would require far-reaching changes in customary American thinking about how education should be structured, controlled, and financed. A key idea discussed at the conference was the "disestablishment" of education—the proposition that Americans should now discontinue the practice of maintaining state schools as they had earlier dispensed with state churches. Not all participants necessarily endorsed this proposal, and it was recognized that the need for continued state financing after school disestablishment would make the parallel with church disestablishment not altogether exact. On reflection, it was also recognized that the American public is still far from ready to entertain a disestablishment proposal. But participants generally brought to the conference a disposition on their own part to welcome far-reaching changes in the present elementary and secondary school system of the United States. (Higher education was not discussed in this conference except through occasional and tangential comments.)

Richard Neuhaus, as director of the conference sponsor, the Rockford Institute Center on Religion and Society, served as discussion moderator, not only calling on speakers in turn but intervening periodically to guide, stimulate, and summarize the discussion.

He opened by stating that the focus of concern was to be the "renewal" of public education. He noted that the conference was bringing together individuals who, while holding divergent opinions in many areas, shared a radical critique of public education. They were generally agreed, he said, that public education had gone wrong to such a degree that the term "crisis" was appropriate, although the present moment held "quite promising" opportunities for dealing with the crisis on the national plane. So, the prospects were not "doleful"—and as it turned out, neither were the conference participants.

Although writers of the papers were to make presentations in turn, and discussion would logically concentrate to some extent on these individually, Neuhaus ventured to affirm that the discussion could proceed on the assumption that all the papers had been read in advance and that all were "in play" at all times. From the outset, then, participants sought to refine and sharpen the total complex of concepts in all of the papers and to reach a clearer understanding of the points on which they variously agreed or disagreed concerning how public education might be renewed and made more democratic.

BEYOND THE ENLIGHTENMENT

Charles Glenn, from the Massachusetts Department of Education's Bureau of Equal Educational Opportunity, led off. He explained that he had sought throughout his entire adult life to work for the rights and interests of poor families and poor children, and that in addition to his professional work in education he served as an unpaid minister in the inner city. But he indicated that in recent years his thinking had been undergoing a change regarding the best way for schools to fulfill their purpose in relation to the poor and to others.

The change, he said, had come in part as a result of his having engaged in a critical analysis of the Enlightenment and its approach to education, in part from some consideration of "neo-Calvinist" thought and the situation in the Netherlands, and in part from his practical experience in a state department of education. He had come to the conclusion that public education policy in the United States, which in large part conforms to the mold established by Horace Mann and others from Enlightenment traditions, had led to development of schools primarily characterized not by hostility to religion but by "blandness and boredom." It has become the case, he said, that "the main mission of a public school official is to avoid doing anything anyone could object to."

"The renewal of education depends on allowing schools to please some parents very much rather than to be forced to avoid displeasing anyone," he went on. Provision should be made, he suggested, for allowing at least some schools to operate with a sense they are not "for everybody." Such a thing is possible in public schools, he promised; in fact, he had seen it taking place in some. While continuing to endorse the effort that had been made to integrate public schools in Boston, he noted that greater diversity and a more distinctive "flavor" could have been permitted. "What about the rights of those parents who don't think their children ought to be told that everybody's views are of equal value?" he asked.

Several conference participants seemed closely acquainted with the school situation in the Netherlands and often made it their reference point in discussions. But Dutch solutions were never cited as a panacea. Indeed, after the umpteenth reference to the Dutch, one participant was moved to wonder aloud if their experience was all that pertinent for Americans. Although the idea of providing government financing for schools operated by people of a specific religious tradition carried strong appeal for conference participants, they acknowledged that the way the idea had worked out in the Netherlands did not necessarily produce the results they desired. On closer inspection, Catholic or Protestant schools did not necessarily give evidence of a particularly discernible Catholic or Protestant character. Although different schools might continue a tradition of serving distinct sectors of the population, that was no guarantee that they would do much to transmit any sense of values or confessional commitment.

From the United States side, Annette Kirk, who had served as a member of the Presidential Commission on Excellence in Education, recalled that in the Catholic schools she attended "we were always more patriotic" than public school pupils—though in some Catholic schools today, she added, the theme seemed to be that everything is wrong with America. Nineteenth-century Protestants such as Horace Bushnell had contended that Catholic schools would build loyalty to Rome and not to America, but an examination of Catholic experience in the twentieth century generally indicates that there is little reason to fear that the state's interest in developing loyal citizens will be subverted by church-sponsored schools.

When some conference participants promoted increased parental control as a path to renewal, Brigitte Berger of Wellesley College urged them to maintain a realistic view of the sorts of values parents actually hold. Though much of the discussion was oriented to concern for parents seriously committed to conveying moral and religious values to their children, she noted that some surveys show many parents simply want their children to be "popular" more than anything else. She cited surveys showing the main interest of students themselves is popularity at age 14 and getting into college at age 17.

Paul Vitz of New York University reported that he had found "home schooling" growing extremely fast in the Midwest, and he suggested that surveys might not be registering the considerable shift among religiously motivated parents toward support for diversity. The Enlightenment tradition, he said, is "more or less played out." Neuhaus suggested that many parents who are now simply "resigned" to the situation would likely "come out of the woodwork" if they were offered a real choice in the kind of school their children could attend.

Stephen Arons, of the Hampshire House Department of Legal Studies at the University of Massachusetts, began by saying that he was not yet ready to reject the Enlightenment. He raised the question of how much diversity could be allowed, and he objected to equating a belief in "some consensus on some items" with support for uniformity. One point he would make mandatory for all schools, he said, was avoiding racial discrimination. But he said the burden should always rest on those proposing such requirements to demonstrate a "compelling" state interest.

Allan Carlson of the Rockford Institute played devil's advocate by asking whether the United States did not need a citizenry with common values and a common "sense of Americanism" to sustain it as leader of the free world. Today the United States clearly faces a greater threat from foreign powers than it did in the relatively more secure nineteenth century. Some people, he acknowledged, would answer that the United States should not play such a role. Although his comments drew little immediate response, there was some discussion of these issues later.

Edward Wynne, professor of education at the University of Illinois in Chicago, then suggested that the nineteenth-century public education theories of Horace Mann could make a positive contribution today in Northern Ireland and Lebanon. He pointed to the large numbers of people in the world's history who had been killed in wars over religion and proposed as a "tactical suggestion" that conservatives today might show more charity in their judgments of people like Horace Mann in past generations. "Maybe their answers were appropriate for that era, and now we're someplace else."

Rockne McCarthy of Dordt College noted that when Thomas Jefferson saw the church establishment coming unglued, he looked for an alternative way of promoting unity among citizens of diverse groups and found it in the common school. McCarthy argued that just as the country learned to accommodate a diversity of churches without anarchy, so it could learn to accommodate a diversity of school systems. True unity is achieved only when a state deals justly with the diverse groups within it, he said.

At this point, Neuhaus intervened to emphasize that the people involved in this conference were not part of some "new right" seeking a return to a "pre-Enlightenment" society. Their concerns, he said, were in fact in keeping with those of such people as Thomas Jefferson, Horace Mann, and John Dewey; it is simply the case that they recognize "a collapse of the secular Enlightenment" and hence want to move on to a "post- Enlightenment" position that will preserve the gains of the past while dealing with a question of injustice that has become "increasingly and painfully manifest."

Pat Lines of the United States Department of Education then made a number of comments she had been accumulating as she listened to other speakers. In a general statement that characterized her contributions throughout the conference, she said that she would "bow out" from the agreement on making a "radical critique." She suggested that the present system is more in need of "fine tuning" than wholesale reconstruction. Noting the earlier reference to the fact that "large numbers" of parents are now educating their own children at home, she said that in relationship to the total population, the estimated fifty to one hundred thousand cases of this sort of home schooling did not in fact indicate "a radically divided society."

Arons next offered a somewhat ironic critique of public schools, saying they were doing "extremely well" in preparing students to operate with the "managerial mentality" that he sees as "the prevailing worldview in the United States." Schools train pupils for service as bureaucrats in the social structures that exist now, he said, whereas the goal should be to enable people to "reconstruct societies." Returning to this point later, he added that the public school "trains middle-class children to be managers" but "sorts out everybody else as those who are going to be managed."

Richard Baer, of Cornell University's Department of Natural Resources, set forth the thesis several times during the conference that public schools operating in accordance with the theories of Horace Mann are in fact not "religiously neutral" but representing a "sectarian position." People who bring a different religious perspective, he said, are treated as minorities and women once were treated: their convictions are dismissed as "private views." As a result of this "overbearing" attitude, he said, "you get read out of the dialogue as a sectarian" just for having a different religious view.

Vitz asserted that dissent from the present system is not limited to the fifty to one hundred thousand families that have taken schooling back into the home but is also evidenced by the large and growing numbers of Catholics, evangelicals, and others who are willing to support alternatives to public education rather than accept the public schools as they are now functioning. "I have to pay—struggling to support a family—thousands of dollars for a public school system that obliterates my heritage, history, values, beliefs, and so on from their textbooks, meanwhile struggling to pay for [my children's] education," he said. "This gets me very angry, and I am not alone." As further evidence of the pervasiveness of the dissatisfaction, he noted that in a recent meeting the Organization of Reformed Judaism had voted approval of religious schools for the first time in its history. The state school is now losing its hold just as the state church did in the eighteenth century, he said.

After a break, the discussion resumed with Berger urging the participants to view the issue not only in terms of schools and the state but also in connection with the central place of families. The public schools do not presently "work" for poor, ethnic minority families, she said, and if the participants were concerned about justice, they should be addressing the injustice inflicted on this class of people.

James Skillen of the Association for Public Justice, commenting on Wynne's proposal to ban sectarian schools in Northern Ireland, predicted that such a move in the present climate would intensify the civil war. He suggested that what Northern Ireland and Lebanon need is not a common school but a government that does justice to the diversity of their peoples. An attempt to impose unity, as the Soviet Union has found in Afghanistan, would not be accepted.

In the spirit of keeping things in perspective, Arons said he empathized with the "quite justified" anger of parents who found schools destructive of their religious values but that for two centuries schools had been destroying the culture of blacks, various language groups, Native Americans, and others. Further, he said, this destruction has been carried out with the complicity of many religious ideologies and institutions, and to some extent it is still fought for by some of the same religious groups protesting the impact of public schools on their own children.

Lines made a related point later in the conference when she observed that although Catholic Bishop John Hughes of New York rightly protested the injustice of the public school system in its treatment of mid-nineteenth-century Catholics, he raised no comparable protest against a much greater injustice American society was then inflicting on another group of people—the slaves. There was little lingering over that point.

Paul Vitz said that he was not himself a fundamentalist, but he had become aware of the extent of fundamentalist anger over the school issue and feared that a social manifestation of that anger "could get scary." Moving toward a new school model could "defuse" the issue, he said, but the absence of any opportunity to talk with the public school leadership about the problem could increase the feeling that the only way to get attention is through violence. "We have a real problem here."

Carlson said that some minority groups have been so devoted to the public schools as a way of getting into the American system that they have traditionally raised no protest about the "destruction of their own cultures." Scandinavian immigrants of the late nineteenth century showed no desire to preserve a Scandinavian culture but rather wanted to "become Americans as quickly as they could," he said. And the immigrants he works with now "love the public schools" as a way of getting into the American mainstream.

John Klenk, an official of the United States Department of Education, suggested that the Enlightenment hasn't yet "played itself out." If it achieved popular support, he said, it would then paradoxically probably be destroyed. But as long as its advocates remain a minority, they will probably be able to continue with a "messianic enthusiasm" on their "elitist" way. They claim to produce republican virtue, though the Great Awakening in the past and black churches today have probably produced more. He also disputed Arons's contention that the public schools are producing "successful bureaucrats." Rather, he said, they give students a "kind of nihilism."

Kevin Ryan of Boston University noted that he had taken his children out of the public schools. He warned that despite widespread dissatisfaction, support for the "idea" of the public schools is so deeply entrenched that persuading Americans to effect fundamental change will be difficult. "Their identity, the identities of their communities, are very wrapped up with the local high school, and it's not going to be dismantled very easily." Recalling his own experience as a student in a Catholic school, he spoke of the fact that "while we knew we were on God's side, we knew that there was something really wonderful and pure about the melting pot idea that was going on in that other school, the public school." That is "very deep" in the American consciousness as a supposed source of unity, he said.

Responding to a question about the role of the state, Glenn said that although it is wrong to take the Jacobin approach of absorbing all society into the state, he still contended in the spirit of "neo-Calvinism" that the role of the state in ensuring justice should not be minimized. He urged that functions such as the certification of schools should be seen to by professional bodies, though he was not insensitive to the possibility that the justice function might lead the state to impose some requirements on religious schools. "There may need to be some movement from both sides toward the middle if we're not going to get out of the business entirely of a national purpose."

Discussion then returned to Carlson's question about education in relation to American national purpose and the current role of the United States internationally. Wynne observed that "an imperial nation does not choose to be imperial" but acts thus in reaction to "circumstances." Rome's imperial purpose, he said, was simply to "keep the barbarians away"; the dominant American purpose is similarly "survival," which is now in question because of international challenges. Meeting those challenges need not entail abandoning the quest for a just school arrangement, he said, but neither should we suppose that merely creating the most just country in the world is "going to persuade the Russians."

Baer argued that Christians ought not to rank survival of a nation as their highest value. Referring to the witness of Dietrich Bonhoeffer against the Nazis, he maintained that if the state is unjust, Christians must continue to uphold the cause of justice. Skillen asserted that if people are not convinced of the Russian threat, forcing them to attend common schools will not change their minds—and if they are convinced, that conviction will be expressed whether or not they have attended common schools.

McCarthy said that advocates of public school disestablishment occupied a favorable position in that they could point to the success of church disestablishment in support of their cause, whereas those who brought about church disestablishment could at that time only point to a "new vision of democratic unity."

What should be said, Baer asked, to those who believe church disestablishment worked because the public schools became an alternative force for national unity? McCarthy suggested that the focus should be on the nature of the political community. Glenn noted that in fact America is now unified less by its schools than by the national television networks, which brought some light-hearted suggestions about disestablishing them. Ryan observed that the educational achievement of schools in serving students is what actually strengthens a nation, and diversity is needed to encourage the necessary excellence.

Citing the experience of Russian dissidents, Berger reiterated the need to emphasize the family and the importance of its role in conveying a religious culture. Glenn responded, "I've long felt schooling matters much less than we think." But although the family probably accounts for as much as nintey-five percent of the influences on a child, he said, the school is "perhaps the ultimate symbolic battleground," and removing schools from the conflict would help millions of currently "alienated" American families.

The morning session ended with Kirk warning that "disestablishment" is a "fighting word" in many circles. Neuhaus added that the "shock" of the proposal would help people understand that the current educational system is "coercing consciences" as the established churches did in the eighteenth century.

TEXTBOOKISH PROBLEMS

During the lunch hour, Vitz reported on a study he had recently completed of public school textbooks under a grant from the National Institute of Education, now the Office of Research in the Department of Education. His overwhelming impression, he said, was "how incredibly boring they were."

After his report, Glenn asked about the focus of political history in the textbooks—whether it reflected a Whig view or some other. Vitz said the textbooks had no general thrust aside from such features as reading feminism back into the career of Joan of Arc and similar historical events and giving a lot more space to Mohammed than to Moses and Jesus. Although the textbooks made some references to religion in past centuries, such as in accounts of the Puritans, none of them gave serious treatment to American mainstream religion in the twentieth century. None of the stories in a sample of third- and sixth-grade readers had religion as a central motif, he noted, and stories about religious holidays dealt with peripheral activities such as food preparation rather than the central meaning of the observances. He also reported that the textbooks contained nothing "pro-business," no Horatio Alger stories of the poor or immigrants who made good in the United States, and no patriotic stories set in periods later than the American Revolution. It is "intellectual dishonesty," he concluded, to portray these textbooks as a reflection of American pluralism.

Carlson asked whether the textbooks contained anything showing a point of view regarding homosexuality. Vitz said he found nothing pro-homosexual, but neither did he find any stories in which babies or children featured positively or any showing the joy of being a parent.

A study conducted ten years earlier, Lines recalled, found that females were seldom mentioned, and when they were included, it was only in traditional contexts. Vitz said the situation had changed rapidly, especially between 1968 and 1974, when many of the texts were rewritten.

Contemplating how to communicate the sense of crisis with sharper rhetoric, Neuhaus suggested that the production of such textbooks by the present educational authorities might be described as "professional malfeasance" and "massive professional fraud." Shying away from rhetoric that sharp, Arons noted that most committees responsible for approving textbooks were still dominated by white Protestant Republican males, so it would be somewhat unfair to pin all the blame on the textbook writers without asking how they came to write what they did and how the material came to be adopted.

"I bear part of the guilt," Charles Glenn acknowledged. He issued some of the first textbook guidelines in the country in 1972, requiring every Massachusetts district to establish a committee to ensure that textbooks gave a fair account of the contribution of all groups. The result, he said, was some "ridiculous overcompensation," in part the result of an attempt to meet the mandate by "subtraction"—that is, by removing whatever anybody found objectionable.

Discussion of the textbook study concluded with Vitz deploring the "mishmash" that resulted from the current process, but acknowledging, "What you do about it, I don't know." Berger then asked whether it really matters. The people writing the textbooks today studied a different kind of textbook, and yet their minds don't appear to have been much affected by the values in them, she said. Vitz responded by saying that it was a "symbolic issue."

THE MYTH OF VALUE NEUTRALITY

The afternoon of the first day was devoted to a discussion of Baer's paper on "the myth of value neutrality." His principal argument is that even if such things as Values Clarification methods and the worst forms of sex education were eliminated from public school curricula, it would be "utterly impossible to have a religiously neutral curriculum." All knowledge is a "social construction," he asserted, and "secular nontheistic beliefs can function as religious beliefs."

Richard Neuhaus opened this phase of the discussion by posing the question "What do we mean by 'public'?" and asking why parents are not recognized as legitimate "public actors" when such matters as censorship in school libraries are at issue.

The U.S. Supreme Court refuses to understand this, Arons suggested, because it can anticipate the consequences that would flow from such an understanding. If it were acknowledged that the selection of textbooks is itself a form of censorship by school officials, he said, then justice would require the United States to "dismantle the entire majoritarian structure of public education." He also said that it is generally—though incorrectly—assumed that "if the majority has made the decision, that does not amount to censorship."

"Censorship is inevitable in raising children," because someone has to sort things out, said Wynne. Baer noted that most Americans are comfortable with the family seeing to such matters. But Berger stated that parents have "abdicated their controlling function to the professionals."

Skillen said that parents without authority should not be able to take school authorities into court over a book dispute. But the problem could be resolved, he said, if parents elected the board members controlling their schools and also had the freedom to put their children in an alternative school when the board ignored their complaints about matters such as libraries.

Baer emphasized that his desire was not to return to something that had worked in the past but to move toward "a new *modus vivendi* that has never been tried" since the establishment of government schools. He said he had no sympathy for fundamentalists and members of the Moral Majority, who he believes are attempting to turn the clock back.

McCarthy raised the issue of parents' opportunity to participate in making decisions at their children's schools in terms of the "actual representation" vs. "virtual representation" debate that leaders of the American Revolution had with the British government. A district school board may claim that it exercises virtual representation for all residents, even though some parents may contend that their views are not represented. Actual representation would entail parents "actually participating" in the decision-making process by selection, he said. Wynne objected that in a school with six hundred students such actual participation would not be practically possible. Baer responded that "All can decide whether to have their child in that school."

Exposing another dimension of the problem, Ryan said that in 1932 the United States had 128,000 school districts, but today, with a population twice as large, it has only 16,000 school districts. This means the interaction of parents and school board members cannot possibly be as strong, he said.

Neuhaus next directed attention to the procedural question of how to move toward implementation of a new policy. Carlson urged that the fears of teachers and their unions must be turned into recognition of opportunities. Wynne objected that proposals in the conference papers sounded "immediate and all-embracing," whereas they should be presented as "incremental" changes. Fewer people, he said, would object to proposals for trying them in some states. McCarthy agreed that change would have to come in increments.

That provided Klenk with an irresistible opening for arguing that the next procedural move should be support of the TEACH bill recently proposed by the Reagan administration. It would change the present Title 1 system, which provides remedial instruction to educationally disadvantaged children of poor neighborhoods, by giving vouchers to parents of the eligible children and letting them use the vouchers in any school they preferred—public or private. Inasmuch as it would aid poor and minority children, the bill is one "everybody can support," Klenk said, and it would "put anti-choice people very much on the defensive because they really don't have a moral argument against it."

It will take a long-term effort to change the ways in which people understand school issues, Glenn observed. He suggested that in the whole country there might be no more than twice the number of people in the room with him then who are seriously wrestling with the issues in these terms, he said.

Arons said he feels that the way the public "thinks about school" should change. If they view schooling as a "process of communication" and a forum for concern with meaning, he said, then the case grows stronger for giving it First Amendment protection and forbidding government "meddling." When schooling came to be defined as a social service, the First Amendment connection began to seem remote. He also suggested that the "common core" of the various clauses of the First Amendment ought to be examined further. He believes that this core is designed to protect a political system. But a change took place, he said in a later comment, when schooling became compulsory and parents lost the right they had previously enjoyed to have their children excused from elements of the curriculum they disliked.

Turning to the issue of finding a strategy for change, Skillen noted that "one thing that works is worth thousands of editorials." As an example, he pointed to the tax credit arrangement in Minnesota and suggested that efforts should focus on implementing other similar plans so that the public could be made aware that alternative choices can in fact work and that they need not pose a threat to society. Practical successes would have more effect, he predicted, than arguments aimed at trying to create a new mindset. He also suggested that the Catholic argument for aid to the "secular" part of parochial schooling was a mistake that reinforced the idea that parochial schools are "private," not "public."

Arons noted that Lenin had taught that the important matter is not who starts a revolution but who gains control once it has begun. Similarly, he said, any plan to change American education today must take account of the "political context" and of such lessons as those to be derived from the 1968 decentralization battle in New York, when the teachers' union was "able to cause it to fail" and thus presumably prove that the experiment "couldn't work."

Berger warned that efforts for change must also take account of another context: the "technological-managerial values" that now hold a strong grip on the core of American society.

Arons turned back to the stark reality that efforts to bring change must confront the vested interests of a $130-billion-a-year industry. Klenk pointed out that it's now $145 billion a year. And with that mantra for meditation, all adjourned for dinner.

THE ISSUE IS JUSTICE

The morning session of the second day was devoted to discussion of Skillen's paper and associated ideas.

Said Skillen, "We are arguing for a disentanglement of the state from education far more than anybody in the mainstream is arguing"—though that is not to say that government should be left with no role at all. The proper task of government, he said, is to provide a "context for diversity," to offer religious services while leaving it to each religious body to determine the content and structure of its services.

Almost immediately the question arose of how much discrimination a school in the proposed new system would be allowed to exercise in admitting students. Everybody appeared to agree that racial discrimination should be prohibited as a matter of course, but there also seemed to be some agreement that other types of discrimination would be necessary and justifiable to realize parental desires. Just where to set such guidelines remained a matter of debate. It was generally agreed that wherever they were set, some schools would likely choose to do without government money rather than abide by them.

Wynne asked whether a school should be allowed to require that parents believe in the Christian faith "and be practitioners." Another type of discrimination, he said, was practiced by a Lithuanian school in Chicago that admits students only if their parents are committed to speaking Lithuanian at home.

Skin color has nothing to do with the educational goals of a school and so should not enter into a decision about admitting students, Skillen said, but a religiously oriented school might well insist that at least one parent share his or her faith with the child so that the home could reinforce the teaching in the classroom. Alternatively, he said, some schools might not want any parental interference in their operations. In general, he suggested, if a school states its philosophy and parents decide that it is what they want, their child should be accepted.

Citing the Dutch experience again, Glenn noted that in two of the confessional schools he visited, only four percent of the students came from families that were actively involved with churches. With that sort of thing being the case, he said, those opposed to the confessional schools have found it strategically advantageous to promote parental involvement as a way of eliminating religious aspects from the curriculum, their ultimate goal being the removal of the confessional identities.

Carlson brought up the issue of the basic strength of the contemporary family and its role both in education and elsewhere. A strong "ideological current" running in the twentieth century is bringing about the "collapse of the family" and the "rise of the state as a substitute parent," he said. In a historical study of the family that was influential some decades ago, he said, Arthur Calhoun identified the family with "the age of savagery" and the state with "the age of civilization." The American constitutional system pays little attention to the family, Carlson continued, relative to the emphasis placed upon it in most Western European countries. He also quoted one scholar to the effect that the American constitutional system gives less protection to the family than to business corporations.

Arons proceeded with a critique of the paper, suggesting that Skillen had made a "large mistake" in speaking of aid to schools, because the Supreme Court had already shown that it would not accept aid to schools that were religious. To avoid the appearance of a church-state "entanglement," he said, it would be necessary to posit a "screen," some person or body other than the state to make the choice of where the money goes, he said, though even such a proposal would have only a slim chance of being accepted. A better approach, he said, would be something like the GI Bill or a system of tuition vouchers.

Identifying a second problem, Arons noted that Skillen left the door open for governmental determination of competency despite the fact that competency testing has often been used as a "back door" way of imposing on home schooling what the state wants to impose in public schools. "I would start with the presumption that the government can make no content requirement in the absence of some compelling state interest," said Arons.

Skillen replied in regard to the first objection that he assumed parental choice would be basically determinative. On the second point, he said that a "compelling" state interest could be invoked against a student emerging from a program of instruction "incompetent to participate in the society." He also indicated an unwillingness to presume that government actions would always and necessarily be "detrimental or at least a threat."

"I do take a fairly thoroughgoing laissez-faire attitude about this, as I would about the government's attempts to control any form of communication," responded Arons. "There are some compelling justifications which the state could advance for certain things." It boils down, he said, to what government would test for. Regarding race and linguistic discrimination, he said, there is no problem, because the justice issue is clear. But history testing "might be very problematic." He also noted that many people in private education oppose vouchers or any other form of aid because they fear government control. There remains the central question, he said, of how to bring about a "change of consciousness" among the general population. Many Americans anticipate "balkanization" and have an exaggerated fear that aid for nongovernment schools would lead to the establishment of institutions controlled by Nazis, the Ku Klux Klan, and other extremist groups. Skillen agreed that an "incremental" approach working through vouchers is the only way his proposed change of systems would occur "in the American context." Baer cautioned that an educational philosophy could not be built on the patronizing view that parents would not be able to prevent bad situations if they were given the opportunity to exercise choice. He likewise warned against allowing educational philosophies to be built only in reference to pathological cases.

Lines noted that a good deal of empirical information about parental choices in education already exists and should be researched. She also recommended focusing attention on countries other than the Netherlands. She warned that instituting a voucher system could bring disappointment if people later found things had remained much as they were before. She also took special note of the religious orientation of much of the discussion at the conference. "I sense an assumption that religion is going to play the main role" in the selection of schools, she said. "I really question that, based on empirical evidence." Although she acknowledged that fundamentalist Christians choose their children's school principally for religious reasons, and for Jews the choice is "probably cultural and religious," she noted that there was reason to assume that Catholic parents tend to choose parochial schools for their "discipline and educational standards." And once religious schools of any sort are established, they "begin to behave like all institutions." She also urged consideration of options other than vouchers—alternatives such as child allowances, tax benefits, and working to correct what is wrong with the public schools. "I don't buy the argument that it is terribly unjust to require somebody to pay tuition and pay taxes too," she said. "My main concern is for parents who don't have the economic means for exercising choice, and they tend to also suffer from other past legal and social discrimination. . . . I also count myself as a political conservative, and I suppose this was a liberal statement."

Contemplating the outcome of government aid also brought an expression of apprehension from Wynne. "In the nineteenth century, Catholics raised a very elaborate school system without any federal money," he noted. If they are not maintaining it today, he said, it is because they are making other choices about the use of their money. "If that's the way they want to spend their money, I don't have a lot of faith in their choices about schools," he said, "because serious schools take very serious parental commitment in one form or another." He also suggested that the proposals for a new system should allow for modification through developments along the way and emphasize that the advocates do not know where "the electorate" eventually will "draw the line."

After a break, Klenk expressed appreciation for the emphasis on justice. But he raised a question about "pluralism" and "New Deal egalitarianism"—two forms of justice coming into conflict in the proposal that private schools receiving aid under the new plan not be allowed to charge additional tuition. "I am curious as to how important this is to your moral scheme of things," he said.

"None of these points are so important in themselves," replied Skillen. "They are put forward to illustrate the kinds of problems that are involved." If students of certain races or classes are turned away through the mechanism of tuition increases, he said, the only school left for some will be the school that has to take all who are rejected elsewhere.

Suppose, continued Klenk, that government support is not adequate in an inner city school created by committed poor parents, but they are willing to kick in an extra two hundred dollars.

"I am not denying that a school would be free to raise other funds," said Skillen.

At this point Neuhaus moved in to advise, "You're borrowing an awful lot of trouble from the future." Many of these questions will not need to be addressed, he said, until, in working out the details of parental choice, "someone screams."

"I sense a kind of unrealism here," said Skillen. He suggested that there is today a widespread conviction in the United States that schooling belongs to government, and it will not be easy to move away from it. To imagine that Americans can be persuaded to move toward "something more libertarian" without taking account of broad questions about the public interest, he said, is highly unrealistic.

"I agree completely with him," said Arons. "Our present system at least attempts to include certain publicly defined ideas of justice in education. We must face the fears and questions that people have about whether a shift to attain the other aspect of justice—equality of choice—is going to come at the cost of these other initial forms of justice."

However, Baer insisted again on the priority of emphasizing the injustice of the existing system. "There is no way to make a government monopoly school system just," he said; "every curriculum will be based on a worldview." And he concluded that "no amount of tinkering with the present system will take away the severe coercion and violation of conscience." Countering an objection that empirical data indicated that many new schools are not worth the trouble, he stated, "Freedom of speech has nothing to do with the fact that ninety percent of Americans never use their freedom of speech very wisely. . . . I haven't felt you've heard the intensity of the argument at the level of principle of freedom of conscience."

Returning to issues of strategy and tactics, Glenn noted that the "freedom of choice" concept in the South had been held unconstitutional, though he held out the hope for progress over the next twenty years if parents continue to pressure their public school systems to provide character and value education in public schools. Many parents have already indicated that they want this sort of thing, and educational bureaucrats will have to recognize, said Glenn, that the only way to accommodate this demand "without endless controversy" will be through offering choice—first within the public school system, and then "increasingly the logic of that, I think, will lead to wider choice."

At several points in the conference, participants referred to work done by Donald Erickson, a professor of education at UCLA, and particularly to his finding that private schools in British Columbia were stronger when they had to support themselves than after they began relying on government funds. Carlson referred to "the black hole of the Erickson argument," that adversity creates a successful school, and raised the question of whether success in changing the U.S. system might have similar "unintended consequences" to the detriment of strongly committed religious schools. In that connection, he also recalled the reports of growing "homogenization" and loss of religious identity in the confessional schools of the Netherlands, and he noted that studies of higher education in the United States had turned up evidence of similar homogenization of state and church-sponsored institutions.

McCarthy then opened up a much broader agenda. "When Jim and I started this work in the area of education, it was certainly because of concern for the justice issue relative to the schools," he said. "But it was also our understanding that looking at that problem would open a window on the much larger question of what is the very nature and task of the state in a pluralistic society." This involves an alternate social philosophy, he said, with changes not only for schools but also for the family, business, and other spheres. But focusing on the state cannot solve all the problems, he said, and specifically it will not "secure good schools"; at best it will increase the opportunities for securing good schools. "Politics is important but it is not everything," he concluded.

Arons called for a strategy with goals not quite so far-reaching as a "second American Revolution," though broader than the particular issue of vouchers. To this end, he made three proposals, suggesting that advocates of change (1) capture the "language" of the debate regarding choice, (2) integrate the education issue with other justice issues, and (3) comment publicly on particular proposals as they come up.

THE STORY OF AN ENCOUNTER

Presenting another dash of political realism, Ryan reminded his colleagues that the nation has two and a half million teachers, and "I've never met one who is in favor of any of these plans." They are afraid, he said, that they will find themselves displaced and looking for work in some storefront school. On the other hand, Skillen observed, the actions of these teachers sometimes give another message, as in the case of the forty-six percent of public school teachers in Chicago who send their own children to private schools.

The morning ended with Klenk asking Skillen if he were not "statist" in relying on the government for justice. Skillen replied that anarchy rather than justice would prevail "in the absence of government." The discussion then drifted into inconclusiveness, except for an observation by Neuhaus that agreeing on the injustice of an existing situation is easier than defining what would be just in the context of American public education.

TO DISESTABLISH OR NOT TO DISESTABLISH

In the final session of the conference, discussion centered on McCarthy's paper, in which he contends that "genuine pluralism demands disestablishment." Current problems, he said, have grown out of issues left unresolved during the nineteenth-century debate over public schools, which was particularly well-defined in the New York debates between public school forces and the Catholic Church. Earlier discussions had dealt with an analysis interpreting the nineteenth-century development as the result of Protestants accepting first the idea of nonsectarian and then of secular common schools out of fears of the large-scale Catholic immigration. According to McCarthy, though the common schools may have gained a monopoloy on government support as a result of hopes that such a system could ensure that these immigrants would be "Americanized," the basic issues of the debate were never resolved. "We're at the beginning of the renewal of a discussion," he said.

In the previous debate, he said, New York governor William Seward recommended that immigrant children be instructed by teachers of their own language and faith. The Catholics, led by Bishop John Hughes, argued that all education is sectarian and that the government should allocate a proportionate share of education funds to Catholic schools. New York secretary of state John Spencer, serving *ex officio* as superintendent of public schools, also saw that education with no stated creeds would nonetheless be sectarian inasmuch as it would represent the views of a particular sector of the population. Hiram Ketchum, a lawyer on the New York City School Board, served as an advocate of "nonsectarian" education, opposing the allocation of government funds to church-sponsored schools. Spencer proposed dividing the city into districts and letting the majority in each district decide on its kind of school. But Ketchum saw that this did not really solve anything, noting that an injustice would be done to children of whichever group was a minority in a given district. "The only way to deal with the justice issue is to rethink the whole majoritarian structure," McCarthy concluded. And justice is the central issue in the whole debate, he said.

Wynne saw a problem in dividing up children of a neighborhood, especially in the elementary years, and busing them in many directions as schools of various religious groups pulled pupils from large areas to get enough for a school. This would lead to "thin" relationships among the children, he said, and loss of many educational advantages possessed by a school closely tied into its "ecological" context.

"Maybe no school is totally just," Lines observed. As soon as two families get involved in a school, she said, dissent emerges; it could happen even within a single family. The fact that public schools have a "financial competitive advantage," she said, does not justify the charge that they constitute a "monopoly," as some conference participants were contending. She also argued that justice does not require that all people see their vision for education perfectly fulfilled. "I am most concerned," she said, "about those who have no legal or economic means to pursue their vision." She also commented, "I have never quite been able to leap from the recognition that there are all sorts of ideologies and values being taught in the public schools to the point that we should therefore subsidize other schools."

To which Baer responded, "If the public schools regularly required evangelical fundamentalist reading and indoctrination, I presume you would have great problems with that. What I am saying is that many of us experience the public schools exactly like that."

"But the public schools did do this once," Lines said.

"That was unjust," said Baer. But the point is that they are conveying values as much today as they ever did—not the values of Horace Mann, perhaps, but values nonetheless—and those values are "offensive to me," he said.

Neuhaus intervened to suggest that perhaps there was a need for a "more precise definition of what is meant by public justice." It does not mean that everybody must find total happiness in all arrangements, he said. Skillen said that it would be impossible to construct a brief definition.

Reacting to the argument against "majoritarianism," Klenk said it was a "rhetorical and polemical error" to concede that the way things go in the public schools today represents "the will of the majority." To the contrary, he said, the schools are dominated by special interests brokered by such groups as the National Education Association who make the false claim that they represent the unexpressed wishes of the majority. The result is that the public schools suffer from "sectarian rule," he said.

"What would we gain if we talked about school policy as a product of special interests?" asked Arons. "I think what we're saying is that this is a subject which ought not to be decided upon by the majority."

"The majority wants free speech," replied Klenk.

"That's not true, but it doesn't make any difference whether the majority wants it or not; they're stuck with it," said Arons. Talking about what the majority "really wants" is "slightly demagogic," he said, and deflects thought from the central question. It entrenches the misconception, he said, that if the majority gets what it wants, the others can "stick it."

Klenk said he does not favor "majoritarianism," but he thinks that advocates of change could "use the democratic rhetoric to delegitimize the current system."

"You sound like Norman Lear," said Arons; in this group that did not amount to much of an accolade. Arons went on to explain that the basic point was not the "bankrupt position" of People for the American Way regarding textbook selection, trying to make the system "truly democratic" and open, because that is still majoritarian. The goal is rather, he said, to end the present system and let teachers make decisions about such things as choosing textbooks in cooperation with families, in somewhat the same fashion that other professionals provide their services to families.

Here Skillen shot a pointed question at Klenk about his role as an official of the United States Department of Education. Was he working for President Reagan's original proposal, elimination of the Department of Education, and supporting the effort to get the government out of education, supporting the cause of disestablishing education? Or was he taking the position that it was his job as a government official to take care of the people's educational needs better than other government officials had taken care of these needs previously? According to Skillen, the objective was not getting government officials to manage education better but overcoming the idea that "the teaching of children is something state officers should do."

Regarding elimination of the Education Department, Klenk said the administration had found that Congress had "no will" to initiate such a move. He said there was also a "dawning realization" that such an action would not truly disestablish the federal role in education but simply move "the pieces" back to where they were when the Department was created—where they "created more mischief." So the idea of eliminating the department was a "dead issue" as far as he was concerned.

He went on to note that his own position called for operations to proceed on two levels. In public discussion he remains "somewhat careful" in the way he treats philosophical issues. But privately he engages in "nibbling away at a false consensus," an effort that involves marshalling "tactical advantages." In pushing the voucher bill, he said, one might emphasize some themes that one would not emphasize if the proposal were for some "perfectly just political order." It was suggested that it sounded as though he wanted both to improve public schools under the present system and work for a different system of greater justice, that he wanted to have it all. He agreed. "We always want it all," he said. "Our involvement in this conference would be on the basis that we believe we can consistently have it all. . . . Some people may point out that there may be some logical inconsistencies in that, and that's okay."

But Skillen continued to press him: "Do you think government is a principal in education?" Neuhaus stepped in to say that Klenk should not be pushed to make statements that might increase the difficulty of his life as an official of the education department. As moderator, he brought discussion back to the question of whether the basic issue was that the present school system constituted a gross violation of "fundamental rights" and whether the answer was disestablishment of the schools.

Wynne asked about the equity of taxing people who have no children in order to pay for the education of other people's children. Neuhaus then pointed out that the analogy with church disestablishment was not exact on this point, because the government did not give religious vouchers enabling all citizens to finance their religion of choice.

McCarthy asserted that the United States had decided against supporting a multiplicity of church establishments by taxation, but it had developed a consensus that taxation for education was "appropriate." Arons suggested that it was "artificial" to isolate a single issue. "If we are going to talk about this in terms of justice, then I think we have to be a little clearer about justice for whom," he said. It could be argued that the present system victimizes teachers, for example, since it demands that they function as agents of a bureaucracy rather than as professionals.

Glenn called for a "conceptual shift" in the way Americans talk about education. Instead of talking about it only as "instruction," he said, they should talk about its role in "shaping values" and building the kind of society they want. This leads, he said, to the argument that choice must be permitted for the sake of concern with character and content.

After a break, Neuhaus returned to the question of prudent tactics for advocates of positions discussed in the conference. "If we push the justice question in those terms, are we simply tilting at windmills?" he asked. "Are we calling for something that begins to look a little kooky? Do we jeopardize hopes for securing justice regarding schooling by pushing in other realms?"

McCarthy replied that the viewpoint he had outlined was the contribution that "one political tradition" wished to make to the public debate, and it would not provide the language for everyone, though it might serve to stimulate people from other traditions to add their unique contributions to the debate.

Arguing that the public schools violate the First Amendment establishment clause is a "fruitful way to proceed," but that does not mean everyone has to accept that argument to show concern about the issue, said Baer. "That may have to remain in the background in any pragmatic coalition-building of people who are concerned about more freedom and choice in education."

Glenn suggested that although some people would start conceptually with the issue of justice and move on to the necessity of choice and the benefits that would come concerning the content of education, a reverse approach might be better suited to getting the support of others. To reach people who get stirred up about the content of public education today, he said, it might be better to point first to the idea that parents should be given choices and then note that ensuring such choice would have the added benefit of serving the cause of justice. But he suggested that public schools could be required to provide more instruction in basic virtue, the effect of which could be to "marginalize the nonpublic school."

Baer countered that even teaching the Decalogue as an approach to instilling basic virtue would depend on the freedom to talk about the preface to the Decalogue, deliverance from bondage in Egypt, and so on. Ethics taught merely as a set of rules is inadequate, he said.

Recalling the fight over slavery as an analogy, Skillen argued that it was primarily an issue of justice, of whether blacks were "property or people." Such issues as the preservation of the union, the future of freed slaves, and so on were involved, to be sure, but the basic issue took priority over all the others. Similarly, he said, education involves many issues, but the central issue is justice. "Every attempt to get at the reformation of education that avoids the fundamental question in public law will not be sufficient," he said. Disestablishment of schools, he said, is equivalent to setting the slaves free; after that basic action is taken, attention can shift to making needed improvements. Without that basic step, he said, talking about such ameliorative proposals as giving the slaves more free time on the weekends is a distraction.

Unsatisfied with that rather sweeping statement, Kirk shifted the discussion back to ways of making improvements in the present system. Parents are most concerned about the question of character, she said, and attention to character education is "absolutely needed," despite the clear dangers of turning such tasks over to agents of the state. The schools have to give some "citizenship" training just to maintain order, she said. Reporting on her work with the Commission, she said that members had decided the main problem in the schools was lack of order. To deal with that, they decided some common understanding of what the schools are about was needed, and so they proposed the idea of a "core curriculum." As a long-term remedy, she said, parents must be made "aware of their duty" to go into the public schools and influence what is happening there. But she noted that Commission members never succeeded in reaching a common understanding of the purpose of education, and they had even less success in reaching a consensus on the traditionally accepted purposes of promoting "wisdom and virtue."

Ryan said there was strong support among philosophers of education "from Plato to Dewey" for defining the goals of education as wisdom and virtue. And he cited statistics from surveys conducted in 1975 and 1980 indicating that 89 percent of Americans favor moral education in public schools (the figure is 83 percent of parents with children in public schools). Although it is dangerous to entrust the public schools with the task of moral education, he said, we cannot close our eyes to the fact they will inevitably have some sort of impact on children's moral development in any case.

Arons stated that that point only served to reinforce his conviction that "monopolistic" control of education by government schools violated the First Amendment. If polls show that an 83 percent majority of the American public is "interested in messing with my kid's character," he said, he wants to be provided with "some choice in a hurry." If not, he will try to "neuter" moral education in the public schools or "attempt to destroy the public education system altogether."

Lenin having earlier been cited, Glenn in fairness recalled Mao's contention that it is necessary to "heighten the contradictions." In that spirit, Glenn proposed heightening the contradictions with regard to schools in order to demonstrate that it is impossible to create "an" order and hence that it is necessary to create a multiplicity of orders, to establish schools that arrive at order in different ways, so that in the end parents will have some choice. He specified that home schooling should also be permitted.

McCarthy agreed that focusing on character education would force the issue of choice, for although 83 percent of American parents may favor character education, they would surely never agree on one particular answer to the question of what sort of character it should be.

Though "heighten the contradictions" may be good ideology, Arons interjected, it is "crappy politics." Supporting character development programs in the public schools in hopes that it will lead parents to an awareness of the necessity of ending the public school monopoly may sound like a promising strategy, he said, but there is certainly no guarantee that it would arouse the hoped-for response. The strategy amounts to "intellectual judo," he said—"good if you can pull it off," but . . . He sounded skeptical of the future of Maoism in America.

Baer then voiced his apprehensions about the people who would be doing the character education in the public schools. "There is an establishment in place of people who will handle these issues, a particular brand of people"—the same people, he said in tones of discomfort, who have been doing dismal things with sex education of late. About 90 percent of the present teachers would have to be shot, he suggested wryly.

"We thought about that," said Kirk, though apparently not in reference to the proposed slaughter. She reported that Commission members first considered requiring the teachers themselves to take courses in character education, but after thinking about the likely nature and content of such courses, they dropped the idea. When Bible reading and other explicitly religious activity was removed from public schools, she said, the "vacuum" was filled with Values Clarification programs. With these now going out, she said, legislators are asking for character education, and certain groups are getting their programs for this adopted. Commission members finally decided, she said, that attempting to teach character directly was "not the way to go." There was talk of teachers serving as "exemplars," but that would entail other problems in a context in which some people are calling for mandatory drug testing for school faculty and staff. "It's gotten so bad you just can't control the exemplar thing any more," she said.

Skillen came back to the idea of heightening contradictions. In America, he said, that leads to "reactionism." But he also expressed pessimism about persuading the general public to support the goals outlined in the conference. He asked whether the argument that participants had been putting forth would not sound so strange to most people that there would be "no point in saying it outside this circle."

Arons suggested that there was merit in making the argument even if it did sound strange. And he proposed that character development could be introduced in a fashion that would heighten contradictions in a useful way, perhaps by introducing it only in private schools and making these schools consequently more desirable.

Klenk objected to the position of those who, out of concern for securing an ideal system, refuse to help people in the present system, or who support the Marxist idea that the worse things are, the better they are, since only crisis can generate change. "Character is going to be taught one way or another," he contended. "So to abandon the notion that we are going to do something about the way character is taught because we cannot agree about how character should ideally be taught seems to me to lack a certain amount of charity. If we take a position that may almost smack of fanaticism, we are not going to have legitimacy and credibility with those people we want to help." Our approval or disapproval of the system should not determine our commitment to serve the people inside it, he argued.

McCarthy objected that he had not heard anybody in the conference suggesting that the people in the system should be abandoned. But Klenk continued, "What do we do now? Say the world is lost? Let's blow it up and recreate the it? That's not a position I can take." He reported more concretely that he had recently been involved in allocating $2.5 million for character education. He defended the action as useful while granting that it was not an "ultimate solution" and that in an ideal world "there would probably not be people like me doing such things." Arons asked if he would vote as a legislator to require character education. He replied that he would.

McCarthy suggested that efforts could be made to improve character education while at the same time clearly aiming toward a new system.

Ryan noted that a 1978 study of forty-four state codes showed that schools had a responsibility for character development in forty of them. And Glenn added that character education was a common aspect of public school teaching until a "loss of nerve" came in the 1960s.

In a renewed spirit of realism, Neuhaus noted the difficulty posed by "cultural erosion" and the lack of widescale outrage among the American people over the school situation. Although "the cornerstone is justice," he said of the proposal for a new system, not many Americans get outraged by the contradiction of justice here. "Not very many Americans really have any beliefs they want to pass on," he said. "Therefore they don't know when their beliefs have been spit upon in school." Something has to happen to bring a revival of culture and renewed defense of perceptions of the true and the good, he said. It will help, he said, to cast the proposal to parents, teachers, and others in terms of "doing justice to you."

Glenn recommended a strategy of presenting "winsome" examples of "flavorful schools." The need, he said, is not so much to define justice in education as to show "visions" of justice.

Baer said he was "depressed" by the number of university students who take it for granted that the state has priority in rearing children. He said they have seen the federal government move effectively for civil rights and justice for women, and in their eyes the justice it has provided compares favorably with the injustice of an Archie Bunker expression of family attitudes. They view the state as a benevolent champion of justice, having no familiarity with the contrary experience in Germany and Eastern Europe of the state as a repressive force, he said.

The way to start, said Klenk, is to show that the present system is "failing to serve the needs of the poor and the minorities." If that can be established, the door will be opened "to a lot of other things," he said. "The debate here would be very, very strange indeed to a lot of people, but if they come to believe there is something unjust about the system in terms of the weak and the poor and so forth, then they will listen to these other things."

Baer underscored the importance of seeking out black and Hispanic support for educational choice. When black leaders decide vouchers represent the way for them to go, he said, it carries particular weight. This met with general agreement, although Kirk wondered whether the focus on coalition-building around choice might be premature. "Before we get to the question of choice, as such," she asked, "don't we have to bring people into some kind of consensus about the purpose of schools as such?"

There was no formal summation at the conclusion of the conference, but Neuhaus did note a number of ideas that had emerged from discussion and had struck him as useful. He also spoke of possible next steps, such as a conference on the relation of the family to democratic freedom. He also took note of the special contribution Arons had made by approaching the issue more from the "secular" perspective of maximizing First Amendment freedom than from the perspective of religious concern that formed a large part of the motivation for many other participants.

The group came to final adjournment with an apparent sense of having spent the time profitably but without any attempt to write a common statement or platform. "It's been a good couple of days," said the moderator. There was ready agreement.

Participants

Stephen Arons of the Department of Legal Studies, University of Massachusetts, and author of *Compelling Belief: The Culture of American Schooling*

Richard A. Baer, Jr., of the Department of Natural Resources, Cornell University

Brigitte Berger of the Sociology Department, Wellesley College, coauthor of *War over the Family: Capturing the Middle Ground*, and editor of *Child Care and Mediating Structures*

Allan Carlson of the Rockford Institute

Tracy Early, free-lance journalist, New York City

Charles L. Glenn of the Bureau of Equal Educational Opportunity, Massachusetts Department of Education

Annette Y. Kirk of Kirk Associates, Inc.

John D. Klenk of the Office of the Deputy Undersecretary for Planning, Budget and Evaluation, U.S. Department of Education

Pat Lines of the U.S. Department of Education

Rockne M. McCarthy of the Studies Institute, Dordt College, and coauthor of *Disestablishment a Second Time: Genuine Pluralism for American Schools* and *Society, State, and Schools: A Case for Structural and Confessional Pluralism*

Richard John Neuhaus of the Rockford Institute Center on Religion and Society

Kevin Ryan of the School of Education, Boston University, author of *Questions and Answers on Moral Education*, and editor of *Don't Smile until Christmas: Accounts of the First Year of Teaching*

James W. Skillen of the Association for Public Justice and author of *Christians Organizing for Political Service*

Paul T. Stallsworth of the Rockford Institute Center on Religion and Society

Paul C. Vitz of the Department of Psychology, New York University, and author of *Psychology as Religion: The Cult of Self-Worship*

Edward A. Wynne of Character II and author of *Character Policy: An Emerging Issue* and *Looking at Schools: Good, Bad, and Indifferent*